# CAMBRIDGE LIBRARY COLLECTION

*Books of enduring scholarly value*

## Religion

For centuries, scripture and theology were the focus of prodigious amounts
of scholarship and publishing, dominated in the English-speaking world
by the work of Protestant Christians. Enlightenment philosophy and
science, anthropology, ethnology and the colonial experience all brought
new perspectives, lively debates and heated controversies to the study of
religion and its role in the world, many of which continue to this day. This
series explores the editing and interpretation of religious texts, the history of
religious ideas and institutions, and not least the encounter between religion
and science.

## The Journal of David Brainerd

David Brainerd (1718–47) was a colonial American missionary to Native
Americans made famous when Jonathan Edwards (1703–58) posthumously
edited his journal and other writings into a popular biographical narrative.
Having spent time at Yale University, Brainerd entered the ministry in 1742
and dedicated his life to work amongst native peoples in Massachusetts,
Pennsylvania, and New Jersey before expiring at the age of 29. This 1902
edition of *The Diary and Journal of David Brainerd* provided readers with
a broader picture of his life and the source material from which Edwards
composed his narrative. Volume 2 focuses mostly upon his work with
Native Americans as well as correspondence and other religious writing.
The thoughts preserved in this two-volume set are an important resource
for those interested in religion in America during the period known as the
'Great Awakening'.

T0381789

Cambridge University Press has long been a pioneer in the reissuing of out-of-print titles from its own backlist, producing digital reprints of books that are still sought after by scholars and students but could not be reprinted economically using traditional technology. The Cambridge Library Collection extends this activity to a wider range of books which are still of importance to researchers and professionals, either for the source material they contain, or as landmarks in the history of their academic discipline.

Drawing from the world-renowned collections in the Cambridge University Library, and guided by the advice of experts in each subject area, Cambridge University Press is using state-of-the-art scanning machines in its own Printing House to capture the content of each book selected for inclusion. The files are processed to give a consistently clear, crisp image, and the books finished to the high quality standard for which the Press is recognised around the world. The latest print-on-demand technology ensures that the books will remain available indefinitely, and that orders for single or multiple copies can quickly be supplied.

The Cambridge Library Collection will bring back to life books of enduring scholarly value (including out-of-copyright works originally issued by other publishers) across a wide range of disciplines in the humanities and social sciences and in science and technology.

# The Journal of David Brainerd

VOLUME 2

EDITED BY JONATHAN EDWARDS

CAMBRIDGE
UNIVERSITY PRESS

CAMBRIDGE UNIVERSITY PRESS

Cambridge, New York, Melbourne, Madrid, Cape Town, Singapore,
São Paolo, Delhi, Dubai, Tokyo

Published in the United States of America by Cambridge University Press, New York

www.cambridge.org
Information on this title: www.cambridge.org/9781108014380

© in this compilation Cambridge University Press 2010

This edition first published 1802
This digitally printed version 2010

ISBN 978-1-108-01438-0 Paperback

## Books for the Heart

*Edited by* ALEXANDER SMELLIE, M.A.

## THE
# JOURNAL OF DAVID BRAINERD

# THE JOURNAL OF DAVID BRAINERD

Volume II

Published by Andrew Melrose
16 Pilgrim Street, London, E.C.
MDCCCCII

# CONTENTS

—◆—

# PREFACE

———◆———

THE design of this publication is to give God the glory of His distinguishing grace, and gratify the pious curiosity of those who are waiting and praying for that blessed time, when the Son of God, in a more extensive sense than has yet been accomplished, shall receive *the heathen for His inheritance and the uttermost parts of the earth for His possession.*

Whenever any of the guilty race of mankind are awakened to a just concern for their eternal interest, are humbled at the footstool of a sovereign God, and are persuaded and enabled to accept the offers of redeeming love, it must always be acknowledged a wonderful work of divine grace, which demands our thankful praises. But doubtless it is a more affecting evidence of Almighty power, a more illustrious display of sovereign mercy, when those are enlightened with the knowledge of salvation, who have for many ages dwelt in the grossest darkness and heathenism, and are brought to a cheerful subjection to the government of our divine Redeemer, who from generation to generation had remained the voluntary slaves of the prince of darkness.

This is that delightful scene which will present itself to the reader's view, while he attentively peruses the following pages. Nothing certainly can be more agreeable to a benevolent and religious mind, than to see those who were sunk in the most degenerate state of human nature, not only at once renounce those barbarous customs they had been inured to from their infancy, but surprisingly transformed into the character of real and devout Christians.

This mighty change was effected by the plain and faithful preaching of the Gospel, attended with an uncommon effusion of the divine Spirit, under the ministry of the Rev. David Brainerd, a Missionary employed by the Hon. Society in Scotland for Propagating Christian Knowledge. And surely it will administer abundant matter of praise and thanksgiving to that honourable body, to find that their generous attempt to send the Gospel among the Indian nations upon the borders of New York, New Jersey, and Pennsylvania, has met with such surprising success.

It would perhaps have been more agreeable to the taste of polite readers, if the following Journal had been cast into a different method, and formed into one connected Narrative. But the worthy

author, amidst his continued labours, had no time
to spare for such an undertaking. Besides, the
pious reader will take peculiar pleasure in seeing
this work described in its native simplicity, and
the operations of the Spirit upon the minds of
these poor benighted pagans laid down just in the
method and order in which they happened. This,
it must be confessed, will occasion frequent repe-
titions; but as they tend to give a fuller view
of this amazing dispensation of divine grace in
its rise and progress, we trust they will easily
be forgiven.

When we see such numbers of the most ignorant
and barbarous of mankind, in the space of a few
months, *turned from darkness to light and from the
power of sin and Satan unto God,* it gives us
encouragement to wait and pray for that blessed
time, when our victorious Redeemer shall, in a
more signal manner than He has yet done, display
the "banner of His cross, march on from conquering to conquer, till the kingdoms of this world are
become the kingdoms of our Lord and of His
Christ." Yea, we cannot but lift up our heads
with joy, and hope that it may be the dawn of
that bright and glorious day, when the *Sun of
Righteousness* shall arise and shine from one end of
the earth to the other; when, to use the language
of the inspired prophets, the *Gentiles shall come to
His light, and kings to the brightness of His rising,* in
consequence of which *the wilderness and solitary*

*place shall be glad, and the desert rejoice and blossom as the rose.*

It is doubtless the duty of all in their different stations, and according to their respective capacities, to use their utmost endeavours to bring forward this promised, this desired day. There is a great want of schoolmasters among these Christianised Indians, to instruct their youth in the English language and the principles of the Christian faith. There is no certain provision made for this at present; if any, therefore, are inclined to contribute to so good a design, we are persuaded they will do an acceptable service to the kingdom of the Redeemer. And we earnestly desire the most indigent to join, at least in their wishes and prayers, that this work may prosper more and more, till the *whole earth is filled with the glory of the Lord.*

THE CORRESPONDENTS.[1]

[1] The Correspondents were the Council in America which supervised, on behalf of the Society in Scotland, the Missionary work amongst the Red Indians.

# THE JOURNAL OF
# DAVID BRAINERD

———◆———

## PART I.

"MIRABILIA DEI INTER INDICOS"; OR, THE RISE AND
PROGRESS OF A REMARKABLE WORK OF GRACE
AMONGST A NUMBER OF THE INDIANS IN THE
PROVINCES OF NEW JERSEY AND PENNSYLVANIA.

CROSSWEEKSUNG, IN NEW JERSEY, *June* 19, 1745.

HAVING spent most of my time for more than a
year past amongst the Indians in the Forks of
Delaware in Pennsylvania, and having in that time
made two journeys to Susquehanna River, far back
in that province, in order to treat with the Indians
respecting Christianity; and not having had any
considerable appearance of special success in either
of those places, which damped my spirits and was
not a little discouraging to me; upon hearing that
there was a number of Indians in and about a place

called by the Indians Crossweeksung, in New Jersey, near fourscore miles south-east from the Forks of Delaware, I determined to make them a visit, and see what might be done towards their conversion. I accordingly arrived among them this day.

Found very few persons in the place I visited, and perceived the Indians in those parts were very much scattered, there being not more than two or three families in a place, from six to thirty miles distant. However, I preached to those few I found, who appeared well-disposed, and not inclined to object and cavil, as the Indians had frequently done elsewhere.

When I had concluded my discourse, I informed them (there being none but a few women and children) that I would willingly visit them again the next day. They accordingly set out and travelled ten or fifteen miles, in order to give notice to some of their friends at that distance. These females, like the woman of Samaria, seemed desirous that others might *see the man that told them what they had done* in their lives past, and the misery that attended their idolatrous ways.

*June* 20.—Visited and preached to the Indians again as I proposed. Numbers more were gathered at the invitation of their friends, who heard me the day before. These also appeared as attentive, orderly, and well-disposed as the others.

*June 22.*—Preached to the Indians again. Their number, which at first consisted of about seven or eight persons, was now increased to near thirty. There was not only a solemn attention among them, but some considerable impressions, it was apparent, were made upon their minds by divine truth. Some began to feel their misery and perishing state, and appeared concerned for a deliverance from it.

*Lord's day, June 23.*—Preached to the Indians, and spent the day with them. Their number still increased, and all with one consent seemed to rejoice in my coming among them. Not a word of opposition was heard from any of them against Christianity, although in times past they had been as opposite to anything of that nature as any Indians whatsoever. And some of them, not many months before, were enraged with my interpreter because he attempted to teach them something of Christianity.

*June 24.*—Preached to the Indians at their own desire. To see poor pagans desirous of hearing the Gospel of Christ animated me to discourse to them, although I was now very weakly and my spirits much exhausted. They attended with the greatest seriousness and diligence, and some concern for their souls' salvation appeared among them.

*June 27.*—Visited and preached to the Indians again. Their number now amounted to about forty persons.   Their solemnity and attention still continued, and a. considerable concern for their souls became evident.

*June* 28.—The Indians being now gathered, a considerable number of them from their several and distant habitations requested me to preach twice a day, being desirous to hear as much as they possibly could while I was with them. I cheerfully complied with their motion, and could not but admire the goodness of God, who, I was persuaded, had inclined them thus to enquire after the way of salvation.

*June* 29.—Preached again twice to the Indians. Saw, as I thought, the hand of God very evidently, and in a manner somewhat remarkable, making provision for their subsistence together, in order to their being instructed in divine things.   For this day and the day before, with only walking a little way from the place of our daily meeting, they killed three deer, which was a seasonable supply for their wants, and without which it seems they could not have subsisted together, in order to attend the means of grace.

*Lord's day, June* 30.—Preached twice this day also.   Observed yet more concern and affection among the poor heathen than ever, so that they even constrained me to tarry yet longer with them ; although my constitution was exceedingly worn out, and my health much impaired by my late fatigues and labours, and especially by my journey to Susquehanna in May last, in which I lodged on the ground for several weeks together.

*July* 1.—Preached again twice to a very serious and attentive assembly of Indians, they having now learned in all respects to attend the worship of God with Christian decency. Between forty and fifty of them, old and young, were now present. I spent some considerable time in discoursing with them in a more private way, enquiring what they remembered of the great truths that had been taught them from day to day; and may justly say, it was amazing to see how they had received and retained the instructions given them, and what a measure of knowledge some of them had acquired in a few days.

*July* 2.—Was obliged to leave these Indians at Crossweeksung, thinking it my duty, as soon as health would admit, again to visit those at the Forks of Delaware. When I came to take leave of them, and spoke something particularly to each of them, they all earnestly enquired when I would come again, and expressed a great desire of being further instructed. And of their own accord agreed that, when I should come again, they would all meet and live together during my continuance with them; and that they would do their utmost endeavours to gather all the other Indians in these parts that were yet farther remote. When I parted, one told me with many tears, "She wished God would change her heart";

another, that "she wanted to find Christ"; and an old man that had been one of their chiefs wept bitterly with concern for his soul.    I then promised them to return as speedily as my health and business would admit, and felt not a little concerned at parting, lest the good impressions then apparent upon numbers of them might decline and wear off, when the means came to cease; and yet could not but hope that He who, I trusted, had begun a good work among them, and who I knew did not stand in need of means to carry it on, would maintain and promote it in the absence of them, although at the same time I must confess that I had so often seen such encouraging appearances among the Indians in other places prove wholly abortive.    It appeared also the favour would be so great, if God should now, after I had passed through so considerable a series of almost fruitless labours and fatigues, and after my rising hopes had been so often frustrated among these poor pagans, give me any special success in my labours with them, that I could not believe, and scarcely dared to hope, that the event would be so happy.    I never found myself more suspended between hope and fear than on this occasion.

The encouraging disposition and readiness to receive instruction, apparent among the Indians, seem to have been produced by the conviction that one or two of them met with some time since at the Forks of Delaware, and who have since endeavoured to show their friends the evil of idolatry.   And although the other Indians seemed but little to regard but rather to deride them, yet this perhaps has put them into a thinking posture of mind, or at least given them some thoughts about Christianity, and excited in some of them a curiosity to hear, and so made way for the present encouraging attention.   An apprehension that this might be the case here has given me encouragement that God may in such a manner bless the means I have used with Indians in other places, where there is as yet no appearance of it.   If so, may His name have the glory of it; for I have learned by experience that He only can open the ear, engage the attention, and incline the heart of poor benighted prejudiced pagans to receive instruction.

FORKS OF DELAWARE, IN PENNSYLVANIA, 1745.

*Lord's day, July* 14.—Discoursed to the Indians twice, several of whom appeared concerned, and were, I hope, in some measure convinced by the divine Spirit of their sin and misery.   They wept much the whole time of divine service.   I afterwards discoursed to a number of white people then present.

*July* 18.—Preached to my people, who attended diligently, beyond what had been common among these Indians; and some of them appeared concerned for their souls.

*Lord's day, July* 21.—Preached to the Indians first, then to a number of white people, and in the afternoon to the Indians again. Divine truth seemed to make considerable impressions upon several of them, and caused the tears to flow freely. Afterwards I baptized my interpreter and his wife, who were the first I baptized among the Indians. They are both persons of some experimental knowledge in religion; have both been awakened to a solemn concern for their souls; have apparently been brought to a sense of their guilt and misery, been comforted with divine consolations, have evidently passed under a great change, and I cannot but hope a saving one.

It may perhaps be satisfactory and agreeable that I should give some brief relation of the man's exercise and experience since he has been with me, especially seeing he acts as my interpreter to others. When I first employed him in this business in the beginning of the summer of 1744, he was well fitted for his work, in regard to his acquaintance with the Indian and English language, as well as with the manners of both nations; and in regard to his desire that the Indians should conform to the customs and manners of the English, especially their manner of living. But he seemed to have little or no impression of religion upon his mind, and in that respect was very unfit for his work, being incapable of understanding and communicating to others many things of importance; so that I laboured under great disadvantages in addressing the Indians, for want of his having an experimental as well as a more doctrinal acquaintance with divine truths. At times my spirits sank, and were much discouraged under this difficulty, especially when I observed that divine truth made little or no impression upon his mind for many weeks together.

He indeed behaved soberly after I had employed him, although before he had been a hard drinker; and seemed honestly engaged, as far as he was capable, in the performance of his work. He appeared especially desirous that the Indians should renounce their heathenish notions and practices, and conform to the customs of the Christian world. But still he seemed to have no concern about his own soul, till he had been with me a considerable time.

Near the latter end of July 1744, I preached to an assembly of white people with more freedom and fervency than I could possibly do to the Indians, without their having first attained a greater measure of doctrinal knowledge; at which time he was present, and was somewhat awakened to a concern for his soul. The next day he discoursed freely with me about his spiritual concerns, and gave me an opportunity to use further endeavours to fasten the impression of his perishing state upon his mind; and I could plainly perceive, for some time after, that he addressed the Indians with more concern and fervency than he had formerly done.

These impressions, however, seemed quickly to decline, and he remained in a great measure careless and secure, until some time late in the fall of the year following, when he fell into a weak and languishing state of body, and continued much disordered for several weeks. At this season divine truth took hold of him, and made deep impressions upon his mind. He was brought under great concern for his soul, and his exercise was not now transient and unsteady but constant and abiding, so that his mind was burdened from day to day; and it was now his great enquiry, *What he should do to be saved.* His spiritual trouble prevailed, till at length his sleep in a measure departed from him, and he had little rest day or night; but walked about under great distress. His neighbours could not but observe a wonderful change in his behaviour.

After he had been some time under this exercise, while he was striving for mercy, he says, there seemed to be an impassable mountain before him. He was pressing towards heaven, as he thought, but "his way was hedged up with thorns, that he could not stir an inch farther." He looked this way and that way, but could find no way at all. He thought if he could but make his way through these thorns and briers, and climb up the first "steep pitch" of the mountain, that then there might be hope for him; but no way or means could he find to accomplish this. Here he laboured for a time, but all in vain; he saw it was "impossible," he says, ever to help himself through this insupportable difficulty. He felt it signified nothing, "it signified just nothing at all for him to strive and struggle any more." And here he says he gave over striving, and felt that it was a lost case with him, as to his own power, and that all his attempts were, and for ever would be, vain and fruitless. Yet he was more calm and composed under this view of things than he had been while striving to help himself.

While he was giving me this account of his exercise, I was not without fears that what he related was only the working of his own imagination, and not the effect of any divine illumination. But before I had time to discover my fears, he added that at this time he felt himself in a miserable and perishing condition; that he saw plainly what he had been doing all his days, and that he had never done one good thing. He knew, he said, that he was not guilty of some wicked actions which he knew some others were guilty of. He had not been used to steal, quarrel, and murder; the latter of which vices are common among the Indians. He likewise knew that he had done many things that were right: he had been kind to his neighbours. But still his cry was, "that he had never done one good thing." I knew, said he, that I had not been so bad as some others in some things, and that I done many things which folks call good; but all this did me no good now. I saw that "all was bad, and that I never had done one good thing" (meaning that he never had done anything from a right principle, and with a right view, though he had done many things that were materially good and right). And now I thought, said he, that I must sink down to hell; that there was no hope for me, "because I never could do anything that was good; and if God let me alone ever so long, and I should try ever so much, still I should do nothing but what is bad."

This further account of his exercise satisfied me that it was not the mere working of his imagination, since he appeared so evidently to die to himself, and to be divorced from all dependence upon his own righteousness and good deeds, which mankind in a fallen state are so much attached to, and upon which they are inclined to place their hope of salvation.

There was one thing more in his view of things at this time that was very remarkable. He not only saw, he says, what a miserable state he himself was in, but he likewise saw the world around him, in general, were in the same perishing circumstances, notwithstanding the profession many of them made of Christianity, and the hope they entertained of obtaining everlasting happiness. This he saw clearly, "as if he was now awaked out of sleep, or had a cloud taken from before his eyes." He saw that the life he had lived was the way to eternal death, that he was now on the brink of eternal misery; and when he looked round, he saw multitudes of others who had lived the same life with himself; had no more goodness than he, and yet dreamed that they were safe enough, as he had formerly done. He was fully persuaded, by their conversation and behaviour, that they had never felt their sin and misery as he now felt his.

After he had been for some time in this condition, sensible of the impossibility of his helping himself by anything he could do, or of being delivered by any created arm, so that he "had given up all for lost" as to his own attempts, and was become more calm and composed; then he says it was borne in upon his mind, as if it had been audibly spoken to him, "There is hope, there is hope." His soul then seemed to rest and be in some measure satisfied, though he had no considerable joy. He cannot here remember distinctly any views he had of Christ, or give any clear account of his soul's acceptance of Him, which makes his experience appear the more doubtful, and renders it less satisfactory to himself and others than perhaps it might be, if he could remember distinctly the apprehensions and actings of his mind at this season.

But these exercises were attended and followed with a very great change in the man, so that it might justly be said, he was become *another man*, if not a *new man*.   His conversation and deportment were much altered, and even the careless world could not but admire what had befallen him, to make so great a change in his temper and behaviour.   Especially there was a surprising alteration in his public performances.   He now addressed the Indians with admirable fervency, and scarcely knew when to leave off.   Sometimes when I had concluded my discourse, and was returning homeward, he would tarry behind to repeat and inculcate what had been spoken.

His change is abiding, and his life, so far as I know, unblemished to this day, though it is now more than six months since he experienced this change.   During this time he has been as much exposed to strong drink as possible, in divers places where it has been moving free as water; and yet he has never, that I know of, discovered any hankering desire after it.   He seems to have a considerable degree of spiritual exercise, and discourses feelingly of the conflicts and consolations of a real Christian.   His heart echoes to the humbling doctrines of grace, and he never appears better pleased than when he hears of the absolute sovereignty of God, and the salvation of sinners in a way of mere free grace.   He has likewise of late had more satisfaction respecting his own state, has been much enlivened and assisted in his work, and been a great comfort to me.

Upon a strict observation of his serious and savoury conversation, his Christian temper and unblemished behaviour for so considerable a time, as well as his experience which I have mentioned, I think there is reason to hope that he is *created anew in Christ Jesus to good works*.

His name is Moses Tinda Tautamy. He is about fifty years of age, is pretty well acquainted with the pagan notions and customs of his countrymen, and therefore the better able now to expose them. I am persuaded he has already been, and will yet be, a blessing to the other Indians.

*July 23.*—Preached to the Indians, but had few hearers. Those who are constantly at home seem of late to be under some serious impressions.

*July 26.*—Preached to my people, and afterwards baptized my interpreter's children.

*Lord's day, July 28.* — Preached again, and perceived some of the people more thoughtful than ever about their souls. I was told by some, that seeing my interpreter and others baptized made them more concerned than anything they had ever seen or heard before. There was indeed a considerable appearance of divine power amongst them at the time that ordinance was administered. May that divine influence spread and increase more abundantly !

*July 30.*—Discoursed to a number of my people, and gave them some particular advice and direction, being now about to leave them for the present, in

order to renew my visit to the Indians in New
Jersey. They were very attentive, and earnestly
desirous to know when I designed to return to them
again.

CROSSWEEKSUNG, IN NEW JERSEY, 1745.

*August 3.*—Having visited the Indians in these
parts in June last, and tarried with them some
considerable time preaching almost daily; at which
season God was pleased to pour upon them a spirit
of awakening and concern for their souls, and
surprisingly to engage their attention to divine
truths, I now found them serious, and a number of
them under deep concern for an interest in Christ.
Their convictions of their sinful and perishing state,
during my absence, have been much promoted by
the labours and endeavours of the Rev. William
Tennent, to whom I had advised them to apply
for direction, and whose house they frequented
much while I was gone. I preached to them this
day with some view to Revelation xxii. 17, *And
whosoever will, let him take the water of life freely*;
though I could not pretend to handle the subject
methodically among them.

The Lord, I am persuaded, enabled me, in a
manner somewhat uncommon, to set before them
the Lord Jesus Christ as a kind and compassionate
Saviour, inviting distressed and perishing sinners
to accept everlasting mercy; and a surprising concern soon became apparent among them. There

were about twenty adult persons altogether (many of the Indians at remote places not having had time to come since my return hither), and not above two that I could see with dry eyes. Some were much concerned, and discovered vehement longings of soul after Christ, to save them from the misery they felt and feared.

*Lord's day, August* 4.—Being invited by a neighbouring minister to assist in the administration of the Lord's Supper, I complied with his request, and took the Indians along with me; not only those that were together the day before, but many more that were coming to hear me; so that there were near fifty in all, old and young. They attended the several discourses of the day; some of them that could understand English were much affected, and all seemed to have their concern in some measure raised. Now a change in their manners began to appear very visible. In the evening, when they came to sup together, they would not taste a morsel till they had sent to me to come and ask a blessing on their food; at which time several of them wept, especially when I reminded them how they had in times past ate their feasts in honour to devils, and neglected to thank God for them.

*August 5.*—After a sermon had been preached by another minister, I preached and concluded the solemnity from John vii. 37. In my discourse I addressed the Indians in particular, who sat by themselves in a part of the house. One or two of them were struck with deep concern, who had been little affected before ; others had their concern increased to a considerable degree. In the evening (the greater part of them being at the house where I lodged) I discoursed to them, and found them universally engaged about their · souls' concern, enquiring, *What they should do to be saved.* All their conversation among themselves turned upon religious matters, in which they were much assisted by my interpreter, who was with them day and night. A woman who had been much concerned for her soul, ever since she first heard me preach in June last, obtained I trust some solid and well-grounded comfort. She seemed to be filled with love to Christ, at the same time behaved humbly and tenderly, and appeared afraid of nothing so much as of grieving and offending Him whom her soul loved.

*August* 6.—In the morning I discoursed to the Indians at the house where we lodged. Many of them were tenderly affected, so that a few words about their souls would cause the tears to flow freely, and produce many sobs and groans. In the afternoon, they being returned to the place where I have usually preached among them, I again discoursed to them there. There were about fifty-five persons in all, about forty that were capable of attending divine service with understanding. I insisted upon 1 John iv. 10, *Herein is love.* They seemed eager of hearing; but there appeared nothing very remarkable except their attention, till near the close of my discourse; and then divine truths were attended with a surprising influence, and produced a great concern among them. There was scarcely three in forty that could refrain from tears and bitter cries. All seemed in an agony to obtain an interest in Christ; and the more I discoursed of the love and compassion of God in sending His Son to suffer for the sins of men, and the more I invited them to come and partake of His love, the more their distress was aggravated, because they felt themselves unable to come. It was surprising to see how their hearts seemed to be pierced with the tender and melting invitations of the Gospel, when there was not a word of terror spoken to them.

This day two persons obtained relief and comfort, which appeared solid, rational, and scriptural. After I had enquired into the grounds of their comfort, and said many things to them, I enquired what they wanted God to do more for them? They replied, "They wanted Christ should wipe their hearts quite clean." I can say no less of this day, and I need say no more of it, than that *the arm of the Lord* was powerfully and marvellously *revealed*.

*August* 7.—Preached to the Indians from Isaiah liii. 3–10. There was a remarkable influence attending the Word, and great concern in the assembly; but scarcely equal to what appeared the day before, that is, not quite so universal. However, most were much affected, and many in great distress for their souls. Some few could neither go nor stand, but lay flat on the ground, as if pierced at heart, crying incessantly for mercy. Several were newly awakened, and it was remarkable that, as fast as they came from remote places round about, the Spirit of God seemed to fill them with concern about their souls. After public service was concluded, I found two other persons who had newly met with comfort, of whom I had good hopes; and a third that I could not but entertain some hopes, whose case did not appear so clear as the other. Here were now six in all who had got some relief from their spiritual distresses, and five whose experience appeared very clear and satisfactory. And it is worthy of remark that those who obtained comfort first were in general deeply affected with concern for their souls, when I preached to them in June last.

*August* 8.—In the afternoon I preached to the Indians; their number was now about sixty-five persons, men, women, and children. I discoursed from Luke xiv. 16–23, and was favoured with uncommon freedom in my discourse. There was much visible concern among them while I was discoursing publicly; but afterwards when I spoke to one and another more particularly, whom I perceived under much concern, the power of God seemed to descend upon the assembly *like a rushing mighty wind,* and with an astonishing energy bore down all before it.

I stood amazed at the influence which seized the audience almost universally, and could compare it to nothing more aptly than the irresistible force of a mighty torrent or swelling deluge, that with its insupportable weight and pressure bears down and sweeps before it whatever is in its way. Almost all persons of all ages were bowed down with concern together, and scarcely one was able to withstand the shock of this surprising operation. Old men and women, who had been drunken wretches for many years, and some little children, not more than six or seven years of age, appeared in distress about their souls, as well as persons of middle age. And it was apparent that these children, some of them at least, were not merely frighted with seeing the general concern, but were made sensible of their danger, the badness of their hearts, and their misery without Christ, as some of them expressed it. The most stubborn hearts were now obliged to bow. A principal man among the Indians, who before was most secure and self-righteous, and thought his state good because he knew more than the generality of the Indians had formerly done, and who, with a great degree of confidence the day before, told me, " He had been a Christian more than ten years," was now brought under solemn concern for his soul, and wept bitterly. Another man, considerable in years, who had been a murderer, a Powwow or conjurer, and a notorious drunkard, was likewise brought to cry for mercy with many tears, and to complain much that he could be no more concerned when he saw his danger to be so great.

They were almost universally praying and crying for mercy in every part of the house, and many out of doors, and numbers could neither go nor stand. Their concern was so great, each one for himself, that none seemed to take any notice of those about them, but each prayed as freely for themselves, and appeared to their own apprehension as much retired, as if they had been every one by themselves in the thickest desert. I believe they thought nothing about any one but themselves and their own state, and so were every one praying apart, although all together.

It seemed to me there was now an exact fulfilment of that prophecy, Zechariah xii. 9–12. There was now *a great mourning, like the mourning of Hadadrimmon*; and each seemed to *mourn apart.* I thought this had a near resemblance to the day of God's power, mentioned in Joshua x. 14. I never saw *any day like it* in all respects; it was a day wherein I am persuaded the Lord did much to destroy the kingdom of darkness among this people.

This concern in general was most rational and just. Those who had been awakened any con-

siderable time complained more especially of the
badness of their hearts; those newly awakened
of the badness of their lives and actions past;
and all were afraid of the anger of God, and of
everlasting misery as the desert of their sins. Some
of the white people, who came out of curiosity
to *hear what this babbler would say* to the poor
ignorant Indians, were also much awakened, and
some appeared to be wounded with a view of their
perishing state. Those who had lately obtained
relief were filled with comfort at this season; they
appeared calm and composed, and seemed to
rejoice in Christ Jesus. Some of them took their
distressed friends by the hand, telling them of
the goodness of Christ and the comfort that is
to be enjoyed in Him, and thence invited them
to come and give up their hearts to Him. I
could observe some of them, in the most honest
and unaffected manner, without any design of
being taken notice of, lifting up their eyes to
heaven as if crying for mercy, while they saw
the distress of the poor souls around them. There
was one remarkable instance of awakening this
day, that I cannot but take particular notice of
here. A young Indian woman, who I believe
never knew before she had a soul, nor ever
thought of any such thing, hearing that there
was something strange among the Indians, came
to see what was the matter. In her way to the
Indians she called at my lodgings; and when I

told her I designed presently to preach to the
Indians, she laughed and seemed to mock, but
went to them.  I had not proceeded far in my
public discourse before she felt effectually that
she had a soul ; and before I had concluded my
discourse, was so convinced of her sin and misery,
and so distressed about her soul's salvation, that
she seemed like one pierced through with a dart,
and cried out incessantly.  She could neither go,
nor stand, nor sit, without being held up.  After
public service was over, she lay flat on the ground,
praying earnestly, and would take no notice nor
give any answer to any that spoke to her.  I
hearkened to hear what she said, and perceived
the burden of her prayer to be, *Guttummaukalummeh
wechaumeh kmeleh Ndah,* "Have mercy on me,
and help me to give Thee my heart."  Thus she
continued praying incesssantly for many hours
together.

This was indeed a surprising day of God's
power, and seemed enough to convince an atheist
of the truth, importance, and power of God's Word.

*August* 9.—Spent almost the whole day with the
Indians, the former part of it in discoursing to
many of them privately, and especially to some who
had lately received comfort.  I enquired into the
grounds of it, and gave them some proper instructions, cautions, and directions.

In the afternoon, discoursed to them publicly.
There were now present about seventy persons,

old and young. I opened and applied the Parable of the Sower, Matthew xiii. Was enabled to speak with much plainness, and found afterwards that this discourse was very instructive to them. There were many tears among them while I was speaking, but no considerable cry. Some were much affected with a few words spoken from Matthew xi. 28, with which I concluded my discourse. But while I was conversing near night with two or three of the awakened persons, a divine influence seemed to attend what was spoken to them in a powerful manner. They cried out in anguish of soul, although I spoke not a word of terror; but, on the contrary, set before them the fulness and all-sufficiency of Christ's merits and His willingness to save all that come to Him, while, at the same time, I pressed them to come without delay.

Their cry was soon heard by others, who, though scattered before, immediately gathered round. I then proceeded in the same strain of Gospel invitation, till they were all melted into tears and cries, except two or three; and seemed in the greatest distress to find and secure an interest in the great Redeemer. Some, who had but little more than a ruffle made in their passions the day before, seemed now to be deeply affected and wounded at heart; and the concern in general appeared nearly as prevalent as it was the day before. There was indeed a very *great mourning* among them, and yet every one seemed to *mourn apart*. Their concern was such that almost every one was praying and crying for himself, as if none had been near. *Guttummaukalummeh, guttummaukalummeh;* "Have mercy upon me, have mercy upon me," was the common cry.

It was very affecting to see the poor Indians, who the other day were hallooing and yelling in their idolatrous feasts and drunken frolics, now crying to God with such importunity for an interest in His dear Son. I found two or three persons, who, I had reason to hope, had taken comfort upon good grounds since the evening before ; and these, with others that had obtained comfort, were together, and seemed to rejoice much that God was carrying on His work with such power upon others.

*August* 10.—Rode to the Indians, and began to discourse more privately to those who had obtained comfort and satisfaction ; endeavouring to instruct, direct, caution, and comfort them. But others being eager of hearing every word that related to spiritual concerns, soon came together one after another ; and when I had discoursed to the young converts more than half an hour, they seemed much melted with divine things, and earnestly desirous to be with Christ. I told them of the godly soul's perfect purity and full enjoyment of Christ, immediately upon its separation from the body ; and that it would be for ever inconceivably more happy than they had ever been for any short space of time, when Christ seemed near to them in prayer or other duties.    And that I might make way for speaking of the resurrection of the body, and thence of the complete blessedness of the man, I said, But perhaps some of you will say, I love my body as well as my soul, and I cannot bear to think that my body should be dead, if my soul is happy.    To which they all cheerfully replied, *Muttoh, muttoh* (before I had opportunity to prosecute what I designed respecting the resurrection), No, no.    They did not regard their bodies if their souls might but be with Christ.    Then they appeared *willing to be absent from the body, that they might be present with the Lord.*

When I had spent some time with these, I turned to the other Indians, and spoke to them from Luke xix. 10.    I had not discoursed long before their concern rose to a great degree, and the house was filled with cries and groans.    And when I insisted on the compassion and care of the Lord Jesus Christ for *those that were lost,* who felt themselves undone and could find no way of escape, this melted them down the more, and aggravated their distress, that they could not find and could not come to so kind a Saviour.

Several, who before had been but slightly awakened, were now deeply wounded with a sense of their sin and misery.    One man in particular, who was never before awakened, was now made to feel that *the Word of the Lord was quick and powerful, sharper than any two-edged sword.* He seemed to be pierced to the heart with distress, and his concern appeared to be genuine. He said, "all the wickedness of his past life was brought fresh to his remembrance, and he saw all the vile actions he had done formerly, as if done but yesterday."

Found one that had newly received comfort, after pressing distress from day to day. Could not but rejoice in and admire the divine goodness in what appeared this day. There seems to be some good done by every discourse; some newly awakened every day, and some comforted. It was refreshing to observe the conduct of those that had obtained comfort; while others were distressed with fear and concern, they were lifting up their hearts to God for them.

*Lord's day, August* 11.—Discoursed in the forenoon from the Parable of the Prodigal Son, Luke xv. Observed no such remarkable effect of the Word upon the assembly as in days past. There were numbers of the white people, Quakers and others, who were careless spectators.

In the afternoon I discoursed upon a part of St. Peter's sermon, Acts ii. At the close of my discourse to the Indians, I made an address to the white people; and divine truth seemed then to be attended with power both to English and

Indians. Several of the white heathen were awakened, and could no longer be idle spectators, but found they had souls to save or lose as well as the Indians, and a great concern spread through the whole assembly. This also appeared to be a day of God's power, especially towards the conclusion of it, although the influence attending the Word seemed scarcely so impressive as in some days past.

The number of the Indians, old and young, was now upwards of seventy. One or two were newly awakened this day, who never had appeared to be moved with concern for their souls before. Those who had obtained relief and comfort, and had given hopeful evidences of having passed a saving change, appeared humble and devout, and behaved in an agreeable and Christian manner. I was refreshed to see the tenderness of conscience manifest in some of them, an instance of which I cannot but notice. Perceiving one of them very sorrowful in the morning, I enquired into the cause of her sorrow, and found the difficulty was, she had been angry with her child the evening before, and was now exercised with fears lest her anger had been inordinate and sinful, which so grieved her that she waked and began to sob before daylight, and continued weeping for several hours together.

*August* 14.—Spent the day with the Indians. One of them who had some time since put away his wife, as is common among them, and taken another woman, being now brought under some serious impressions, was much concerned about that affair in particular. He seemed fully convinced of the wickedness of that practice, and earnestly desirous to know what God would have him do in his present circumstances. When the law of God respecting marriage had been explained, and the cause of his leaving his wife enquired into; and when it appeared she had given him no just occasion by unchastity to desert her, and that she was willing to forgive his past misconduct, and to live peaceably with him for the future, and that she moreover insisted on it as her right to enjoy him; he was then told that it was his indispensable duty to renounce the woman he had last taken, and receive the other who was his proper wife, and live peaceably with her during life. With this he readily and cheerfully complied, publicly renouncing the woman he had last taken, and promising to live with and be kind to his wife during life, she also promising the same to him. This afforded a clear demonstration of the power of God's Word upon their hearts. I suppose a few weeks before, the whole world could not have persuaded this man to a compliance with Christian rules in this affair.

I was not without fears, lest this proceeding might be like putting *new wine into old bottles*, and that some might be prejudiced against Christianity, when they saw the overtures made by it. But the man being much concerned about the matter, the determination of it could be deferred no longer, and it seemed to have a good effect among the Indians, who generally owned that the laws of Christ were good and right respecting marriage.

In the afternoon I preached to them from the apostle's discourse to Cornelius, Acts x. 34. There was some affectionate concern among them, though not equal to what appeared in several of the former days. They still attended and heard as for their lives, and the Lord's work seemed still to be promoted among them.

*August* 15. — Preached from Luke iv. 16–21. The Word was attended with power upon the hearts of the hearers. There was much concern, many tears, and affecting cries among them, and some in a special manner were deeply wounded and distressed. There were some newly awakened who came but this week, and convictions seemed to be promoted in others. Those who had received comfort were likewise refreshed and strengthened, and the work of grace appeared to advance in all respects. The passions of the congregation in general were not so much moved as in some days past, but their hearts seemed as solemnly and deeply affected with divine truths as ever, at least in many instances, although the concern did not seem to be so universal, and to reach every individual in such a manner as it had appeared to do some days before.

*August* 16.—Spent considerable time in conversing privately with several of the Indians. Found one that had got relief and comfort, and could not but hope, when I came to discourse particularly with her, that her comfort was of the right kind. In the afternoon I preached from John vi. 26–34. Toward the close of my discourse, divine truth was attended with considerable power upon the audience ; more especially after public service was over, when I addressed several distressed persons.

A great concern spread pretty generally among them. Two persons especially were awakened to a sense of their sin and misery, one of whom was lately come, and the other had all along been very attentive, but could never before obtain any lively view of her perishing state. But now her concern and spiritual distress were such that I had never seen any more pressing. Sundry old men were also in distress for their souls, so that they could not refrain from weeping and crying out aloud ; and their bitter groans were the most convincing as well as affecting evidence of the reality and depth of their inward anguish. God is powerfully at work among them. True and genuine convictions of sin are daily promoted in many instances, and some are newly awakened from time to time ; although some few, who felt a commotion in their passions in days past, seem now to discover that their hearts were never duly affected. I never saw the work of God appear so independent of means as at this time. I discoursed to the people on what I hoped had a proper tendency to promote conviction; but God's manner of working upon them appeared so entirely supernatural and above means that I could scarcely believe He used me as an instrument, or what I spake as means of carrying on His work; for it seemed, as I thought, to have no connection with nor dependence upon means in any respect. And though I could not but continue to use the means I thought proper for the promotion of the work, yet God appeared to work entirely without them; so that I seemed to do nothing, and indeed to have nothing to do, but to *stand still and see the salvation of God*. I was obliged and delighted to say, *Not unto us*, not unto instruments and means, *but to Thy name be glory*. The Lord appeared to work entirely alone, and I saw no room to attribute any part of this work to any created arm.

*August* 17.—Spent much time in private conferences with the Indians. Found one who had newly obtained relief and comfort, after a long season of spiritual trouble and distress. He had been one of my hearers at the Forks of Delaware for more than a year, and now followed me here under deep concern for his soul. I had abundant reason to hope that his comfort was well-grounded.

Afterwards discoursed publicly from Acts viii. 29–39; and took occasion to treat concerning baptism, in order to their being instructed and prepared to partake of that ordinance. They were yet hungry and thirsty for the Word of God, and appeared unwearied in their attendance upon it.

*Lord's day, August* 18.—Preached in the forenoon to an assembly of white people, made up of Presbyterians, Baptists, Quakers. Afterwards preached to the Indians from John vi. 35–40. Considerable concern was visible among them, though not equal to what has frequently appeared of late.

*August* 19. — Preached from Isaiah lv. 1. The Word was attended with power upon those who had received comfort, and others also. The former were sweetly melted and refreshed with divine invitations, the latter much concerned for their souls, that they might obtain an interest in the glorious provisions of the Gospel which were set before them. There were numbers of poor *impotent* souls that waited at the pool for healing, and *the Angel* seemed, as at other times of late, *to trouble the waters.* There was a most desirable and comfortable prospect of the spiritual recovery of diseased perishing sinners.

*August* 23.—Spent some time with the Indians in private discourse ; afterwards preached to them from John vi. 44–50. There was as usual great attention and affection among them. Several

appeared deeply concerned for their souls, and
could not but express their inward anguish by
tears and cries. But the amazing divine influence
that has been so powerfully among them in general
seems at present in some degree abated, at least in
regard to its universality; though many that have
got no special comfort still retain deep impressions
of divine things.

*August* 24.—Spent the forenoon in discoursing
to some of the Indians, in order to their receiving
baptism. When I had opened the nature of the
ordinance, the obligations attending it, the duty
of devoting ourselves to God in it, and the privilege
of being in covenant with Him, several of them
seemed to be filled with love to God, and delighted
with the thoughts of giving up themselves to Him
in that solemn and public manner. They were
melted and refreshed with the hopes of enjoying
the blessed Redeemer.

Afterwards I discoursed publicly from 1 Thessa-
lonians iv. 13–17. There was a solemn attention,
and some visible concern and affection in the time
of public service, which was afterwards increased
by some further exhortation to come to Christ, and
give up their hearts to Him, that they might be
fitted to ascend up and meet Him in the air, when
*He shall descend with a shout and the voice of the
archangel.*

There were several Indians newly come, who
thought their state good and themselves happy,

because they had sometimes lived with the white
people under Gospel light. They had learned to
read, were civil, and such like, but appeared utter
strangers to their own hearts, and altogether unacquainted with the power of religion as well as
with the doctrines of grace. With those I discoursed particularly after public worship, and was
surprised to see their self-righteous disposition,
their strong attachment to the covenant of works for
salvation, and the high value they put upon their
supposed attainments. After much discourse, one
appeared in a measure convinced, that *by the deeds
of the law no flesh living should be justified,* and wept
bitterly, enquiring *what he must do to be saved.*
This was very comfortable to others, who had
gained some experimental acquaintance with their
own hearts; for, before, they were grieved with
the conversation and conduct of these new-comers,
who boasted of their knowledge and thought well
of themselves, but evidently discovered to those
that had any experience of divine truths that they
knew nothing of their own hearts.

*Lord's day, August 25.*—Preached in the forenoon
from Luke xv. 3–7. There being a multitude of
white people present, I made an address to them
at the close of my discourse to the Indians; but
could not so much as keep them orderly. Scores
of them kept walking and gazing about, and behaved more indecently than any Indians I ever
addressed. A view of their abusive conduct so

sank my spirits, that I could scarcely go on with my work.

In the afternoon discoursed from Revelation iii. 20. The Indians behaved seriously, though many others were vain.    Afterwards baptized    twenty - five of the Indians, fifteen adults and ten children. Most of the adults I hope are really renewed ; and there was not one of them but what I entertained some hopes of in that respect, though the case of two or three appeared more doubtful.

After the crowd of spectators was gone, I called the baptized persons together, and discoursed to them in particular, at the same time inviting others to attend.    I reminded them of the solemn obligations they were now under to live to God, warned them of the evil and dreadful consequences of careless living, especially after this public profession of Christianity ; gave them directions for their future conduct, and encouraged them to watchfulness and devotion, by setting before them the comfort and happy conclusion of a religious life.    This was a delightful season indeed.    Their hearts were engaged and cheerful in duty, and they rejoiced that they had in a public and solemn manner dedicated themselves to God.    Love seemed to reign among them.    They took each other by the hand with tenderness and affection, as if their hearts were knit together, while I was discoursing to them.    Their deportment toward each other was such that a serious spectator might justly be excited to cry out with admiration, *Behold how they love one another!* Several other Indians, seeing and hearing these things, were much affected and wept bitterly, longing to be partakers of the same joy and comfort that these discovered by their very countenances as well as conduct.

*August* 26.—Preached to my people from John vi. 51–55. After I had discoursed some time, I addressed those in particular who entertained hopes that they were *passed from death to life*. Opened to them the persevering nature of those consolations Christ gives His people, which I trusted He had bestowed upon some in that assembly ; showed them that such have already the beginnings of *eternal life* (verse 54) and that their heaven shall speedily be completed.

I no sooner began to discourse in this strain than the dear Christians in the congregation began to be melted with desire after the enjoyment of Christ and of a state of perfect purity. They wept affectionately and yet joyfully ; their tears and sobs discovered brokenness of heart, and yet were attended with real comfort and satisfaction. This humble melting state of mind appeared to be the genuine effect of a *spirit of adoption,* and was very far from that *spirit of bondage* that they not long since laboured under. The influence seemed to spread through the whole assembly, and there quickly appeared a wonderful concern among them.

Many who had not yet found Christ as an all-sufficient Saviour were now engaged in seeking after Him. Their number was now about ninety-five, old and young, almost all affected either with joy in Christ Jesus or with the utmost concern to obtain an interest in Him.

Being fully convinced it was now my duty to take a journey far back to the Indians on Susquehanna River (it being now a proper season of the year to find them generally at home), after having spent some hours in public and private discourses with my people, I told them that I must now leave them for the present, and go to their brethren far remote and preach to them; that I wanted the Spirit of God should go with me, without whom nothing could be done to any good purpose among the Indians, as they themselves had had opportunity to see and observe by the barrenness of our meetings at some times, when there was much pains taken to affect and awaken sinners, and yet to little or no purpose. I also asked them, if they could not be willing to spend the remainder of the day in prayer for me, that God would go with me and succeed my endeavours for the conversion of those poor souls. They cheerfully complied with the motion, and soon after I left them (the sun being then about an hour and a half high at night) they began, and continued praying all night till nearly break of day, not suspecting till they went out and viewed the stars, and saw the morning-star a considerable height, that it was later than common bed-time. Thus eager and unwearied were they in devotions. A remarkable night it was, attended, as my interpreter tells me, with a powerful influence upon those who were yet under concern, as well as those who had received comfort.

This day two distressed souls were brought I trust to the enjoyment of solid comfort in Him in whom the weary find rest. It was likewise remarkable that this day an old Indian, who has all his days been an obstinate idolater, was brought to give up his rattles (which they use for music in their idolatrous feasts and dances) to the other Indians, who quickly destroyed them. This was done without any attempt of mine in the affair, for I said nothing to him about it. It seemed to be nothing but the power of God's Word, without any particular application to this sin, that produced this effect. Thus God has begun, thus He has hitherto surprisingly carried on, a work of grace amongst these Indians. May the glory be ascribed to Him, who is the sole Author of it !

FORKS OF DELAWARE, IN PENNSYLVANIA, 1745.

*Lord's day, September* 1.—Preached to the Indians here from Luke xiv. 16–23. The Word appeared to be attended with some power, and caused some tears in the assembly. Afterwards preached to a number of white people present, and observed many of them in tears, and some who had formerly been as careless and unconcerned about religion perhaps as the Indians. Towards night discoursed to the Indians again, and perceived a greater attention, and more visible concern among them than has been usual in these parts.

*September* 3. — Preached to the Indians from Isaiah liii. 3–6. The divine presence seemed to be in the midst of the assembly, and a considerable concern was visible. Several persons seemed to be awakened, amongst whom were two stupid creatures that I could scarcely ever before keep awake while I was preaching. Could not but rejoice at this appearance of things, though at the same time I could not but fear lest the concern they at present manifested might prove like *a morning-cloud*, as something of that nature had formerly done in these parts.

*September* 5.—Discoursed to the Indians from the Parable of the Sower, and afterwards conversed with a few individuals, who wept and cried out in an affecting manner. Others were filled with surprise and concern, and a divine power accompanied what was then spoken. Several of these persons had been with me to Crossweeksung, and had there seen, and some of them, I trust, felt, the power of God's Word in an effectual and saving manner. I asked one of them who had obtained comfort, and given hopeful evidences of being truly religious, why he wept. He replied, " When he

thought how Christ was slain like a lamb and spilt
His blood for sinners, he could not help crying
when he was all alone." He then burst out into
tears and cries again. I then asked his wife, who
had likewise been abundantly comforted, wherefore
she cried. She answered, "She was grieved that
the Indians here would not come to Christ, as well
as those at Crossweeksung." I asked her if she
found a heart to pray for them, and whether Christ
had seemed to be near to her of late in prayer as
in time past—(which is my usual method of ex-
pressing a sense of divine presence). She replied,
"Yes, He had been near to her; and that at some
times when she had been praying alone, her heart
loved to pray so that she could not bear to leave
the place, but wanted to stay and pray longer."

*September* 7.—Preached to the Indians from John
vi. 35–39. There was not so much appearance of
concern among them as at several other times of
late, yet they appeared serious and attentive.

*Lord's day, September* 8. — Discoursed to the
Indians in the forenoon from John xii. 44–50. In
the afternoon from Acts ii. 36–39. The Word of
God at this time seemed to fall with weight and
influence upon them. There were but few present,
but most of them were in tears, and several cried
out under distressing concern for their souls. One
man was considerably awakened, who never before
discovered any concern for his soul. There appeared a remarkable work of the divine Spirit

among them, almost generally, not unlike what has been of late at Crossweeksung. It seemed as if the divine influence had spread from thence to this place; although something of it appeared here in the awakening of my interpreter, his wife, and some few others.

Some of the careless white people now present were awakened, or at least startled, seeing the power of God so prevalent among the Indians. I then made a particular address to them, which seemed to produce some impression upon them. There are several Indians in these parts who have always refused to hear me preach, and have been enraged against those that have attended my preaching. But of late they are more bitter than ever, scoffing at Christianity, and sometimes asking my hearers, "How often they have cried"; and "whether they have not now cried enough." So that they have already *trial of cruel mockings*.

*September* 9.—Left the Indians in the Forks of Delaware, and set out on a journey towards Susquehanna River, directing my course towards the Indian town more than a hundred and twenty miles westward from the Forks. Travelled about fifteen miles, and there lodged.

*September* 13.—After having lodged out three nights, arrived at the Indian town I aimed at on Susquehanna, called Shaumoking (one of the places, and the largest of them, that I visited in May last), and was kindly received and entertained by the Indians; but had little satisfaction on account of the heathenish dance and revel they then held in the house where I was obliged to lodge, which I could not suppress, though I often entreated them to desist for the sake of one of their own friends who was then sick in the house, and whose disorder was much aggravated by the noise.   Alas, how destitute of *natural affection* are these poor uncultivated pagans; although they seem somewhat kind in their own way.   Of a truth, *the dark corners of the earth are full of the habitations of cruelty.*

This town, as I observed in my Journal of May last, lies partly on the east side of the river, partly on the west, and partly on a large island in it.   It contains upwards of fifty houses, and, they tell me, near three hundred persons, though I never saw much more than half that number in it.   But it consists of three different tribes of Indians, speaking three languages wholly unintelligible to each other.   About one half of its inhabitants are Delawares; the others are called Senakas and Tutelas.   The Indians of this place are counted the most drunken, mischievous, and ruffianly of any in these parts; and Satan seems to have his seat in this town in an eminent manner.

*September* 14.—Visited the Delaware king, who was supposed to be at the point of death when I was here in May last, but was now recovered. I discoursed with him and others respecting Christianity; spent the afternoon with them, and had more encouragement than I expected. The king appeared kindly disposed and willing to be instructed; this gave me some encouragement that God would open an *effectual door* for my preaching the Gospel here, and set up His kingdom in this place. It was a support and refreshment to me in the wilderness, and rendered my solitary circumstances comfortable and pleasant.

*Lord's day, September* 15.—Visited the chief of the Delawares again; was kindly received by him, and discoursed to the Indians in the afternoon. Still entertained hopes that God would open their hearts to receive the Gospel, though many of them were so drunk from day to day that I could get no opportunity to speak to them. Towards night, discoursed with one that understood the languages of the Six Nations, as they are usually called, who discovered an inclination to hearken to Christianity; which gave me some hopes that the Gospel might hereafter be sent to those nations far remote.

*September* 16. — Spent the forenoon with the Indians, endeavouring to instruct them from house to house, and to engage them, as far as I could, to be friendly to Christianity. Towards night, went to one part of the town where they were sober, and got together nearly fifty persons, and discoursed to them, having first obtained the king's cheerful consent. There was a surprising attention among them, and they manifested a considerable desire of being further instructed. One or two seemed to be touched with some concern for their souls, and appeared well pleased with some conversation in private, after I had concluded my public discourse. My spirits were much refreshed with this appearance of things, and I could not but return with my interpreter (having no other companion in this journey) to my poor hard lodgings, rejoicing in hope that God designed to set up His kingdom here, where Satan now reigns in the most eminent manner; and found uncommon freedom in addressing the Throne of Grace for the accomplishment of so great and glorious a work.

*September* 17.—Spent the forenoon in visiting and discoursing to the Indians. About noon left Shaumoking (most of the Indians going out this day on their hunting design), and travelled down the river south-westward.

*September* 19.—Visited an Indian town called Juneauta, situate on an island in Susquehanna. Was much discouraged with the temper and behaviour of the Indians here, although they appeared friendly when I was with them the last spring, and then gave me encouragement to come and see them again. But they now seemed resolved to retain their pagan notions, and persist in their idolatrous practices.

*September* 20.—Visited the Indians again at Juneauta Island, and found them almost universally very busy in making preparations for a great sacrifice and dance. Had no opportunity to get them together in order to discourse with them about Christianity, because they were so much engaged about their sacrifice. My spirits were much sunk with a prospect so very discouraging, especially seeing I had now no interpreter but a pagan, who was as much attached to idolatry as any of them (my own interpreter having left me the day before, being obliged to attend upon some important business elsewhere, and knowing that he could neither speak nor understand the language of *these* Indians); so that I was under the greatest disadvantages imaginable. However, I attempted to discourse privately with some of them, but without any appearance of success; notwithstanding I still tarried with them.

In the evening they met together, near a hundred of them, and danced round a large fire, having prepared ten fat deer for the sacrifice. The fat of the inwards they burnt in the fire while they were dancing; sometimes they raised the flame to a prodigious height, yelling and shouting in such a manner that they might easily have been heard two miles or more. They continued their sacred dance all night, or nearly so; after which they ate the flesh of the sacrifice, and so retired each one to his lodging. I enjoyed little satisfaction this night, being entirely alone on the island as to any Christian company, and in the midst of this idolatrous revel. Having walked to and fro till body and mind were pained and much oppressed, I at length crept into a little crib made for corn, and there slept on the poles.

*Lord's day, September 22.*—Spent the day with the Indians on the island. As soon as they were well up in the morning, I attempted to instruct them, and laboured for that purpose to get them together, but quickly found they had something else to do; for near noon they gathered together all their Powwows, and set about half a dozen of them to playing their juggling tricks, and acting their frantic distracted postures, in order to find out why they were then so sickly upon the island, numbers of them being at that time disordered with a fever and bloody flux. In this exercise they were engaged for several hours, making all the wild, ridiculous, and distracted motions imaginable; sometimes singing, sometimes howling, sometimes extending their hands to the utmost stretch, spreading all their fingers, and seemed to push with them, as if they designed to fright something away, or at least keep it off at arms-end; sometimes stroking their faces with their hands, then spurting water as fine as mist; sometimes sitting flat on the earth, then bowing down their faces to the ground; wringing their sides, as if in pain and anguish, twisting their faces and turning up their eyes.

Their monstrous actions tended to excite ideas of horror, and seemed to have something in them peculiarly suited to demon worship. Some of

them, I could observe, were much more fervent
and devout in the business than others, and seemed
to chant, *peep and mutter*, with a great degree of
warmth and vigour, as if determined to awaken
and engage the powers below. I sat at the
distance of about thirty feet from them, undis-
covered, with my Bible in my hand, resolving if
possible to spoil their sport, and prevent their
receiving any answers from the infernal world. I
sat and viewed the whole scene. They continued
their hideous charms and incantations for more
than three hours, till they had all wearied themselves out, although they had in that space of
time taken sundry intervals of rest. At length
they broke up, without appearing to receive any
answer.

After they had done powwowing, I attempted
to discourse with them about Christianity; but
they soon scattered, and gave me no opportunity
for anything of that nature. A view of these
things, while I was entirely alone in the wilderness,
destitute of the society of any one that so much as
*named the name of Christ,* greatly sank my spirits,
gave me the most gloomy turn of mind imaginable,
almost stripped me of all resolution and hope
respecting further attempts for propagating the
Gospel and converting the pagans, and rendering
this the most burdensome and disagreeable Sabbath
that ever I saw. Nothing, I can truly say, sank
and distressed me like the loss of my hope respect-

ing their conversion. This concern appeared so great and so much my own, that I seemed to have nothing to do on earth if this failed. A prospect of the greatest success in the saving conversion of souls under Gospel light would have done little or nothing towards compensating for the loss of my hope in this respect; and my spirits now were so damped and depressed, that I had no heart nor power to make any further attempts among them for that purpose; nor could I possibly recover my hope, resolution, and courage, by the utmost of my endeavours.

Many of the Indians of this island understand the English language very well, having formerly lived in some part of Maryland, among or near the white people; but they are very vicious, drunken, and profane, although not so savage as those who have less acquaintance with the English. Their customs in divers respects differ from those of other Indians upon this river. They do not bury their dead in a common form, but let their flesh consume above ground in close cribs made for that purpose; and at the end of a year, or perhaps sometimes a longer space of time, they take the bones, when the flesh is all consumed, and wash and scrape them, and afterwards bury them with some ceremony. Their method of charming or conjuring over the sick seems somewhat different from that of other Indians, though for substance the same; and the whole of it, among these and

others, is perhaps an imitation of what seems, by
Naaman's expression, 2 Kings v. 11, to have been
the custom of the ancient heathens. For it seems
chiefly to consist in *striking their hands* over the
diseased, repeatedly stroking them, *and calling
upon their gods,* excepting the spurting of water
like a mist, and some other frantic ceremonies
common to the other conjurations, which I have
already mentioned.

When I was in these parts in May last, I had an
opportunity of learning many of the notions and
customs of the Indians, as well as of observing
many of their practices. I then travelled more
than a hundred and thirty miles upon the river
above the English settlements, having in that
journey a view of some persons of seven or eight
distinct tribes, speaking so many different languages.
But of all the sights I ever saw among them, or
indeed anywhere else, none appeared so frightful
or so near akin to what is usually imagined of
infernal powers, none ever excited such images of
terror in my mind, as the appearance of one who
was a devout and zealous reformer, or rather
restorer of what he supposed was the ancient
religion of the Indians.

He made his appearance in his pontifical garb,
which was a coat of bears' skins, dressed with the
hair on, and hanging down to his toes; a pair of
bear-skin stockings, and a great wooden face,
painted the one half black and the other tawny,

about the colour of an Indian's skin, with an extravagant mouth, cut very much awry; the face fastened to a bearskin cap, which was drawn over his head. He advanced toward me with the instrument in his hand that he used for a piece of wood, which made a very convenient handle. As he came forward, he beat his tune with the rattle, and danced with all his might, but did not suffer any part of his body, not so much as his fingers, to be seen; and no man would have guessed by his appearance and actions that he could have been a human creature, if they had not had some intimation of it otherwise. When he came near me, I could not but shrink away from him, although it was then noon-day, and I knew who it was, his appearance and gestures were so prodigiously frightful. He had a house consecrated to religious uses, with divers images cut out upon the several parts of it; I went in and found the ground beat almost as hard as a rock with their frequent dancing in it. I discoursed with him about Christianity; some of my discourse he seemed to like, but some of it he disliked entirely. He told me that God had taught him his religion, and that he never would turn from it, but wanted to find some that would join heartily with him in it; for the Indians, he said, were grown very degenerate and corrupt. He had thoughts, he said, of leaving all his friends, and travelling abroad, in order to find some that would join with him; for he believed

God had some good people somewhere that felt as he did. He had not always, he said, felt as he now did, but had formerly been like the rest of the Indians, until about four or five years before that time. Then, he said, his heart was very much distressed, so that he could not live among the Indians, but went away into the woods, and lived alone for some months. At length, he says, God comforted his heart, and showed him what he should do; and since that time he had known God and tried to serve Him, and loved all men, be they who they would, so as he never did before.

He treated me with uncommon courtesy, and seemed to be hearty in it. I was told by the Indians that he opposed their drinking strong liquor with all his power; and, if at any time he could not dissuade them from it by all he could say, he would leave them and go crying into the woods. It was manifest he had a set of religious notions that he had examined for himself, and not taken for granted upon bare tradition; and he relished or disrelished whatever was spoken of a religious nature, according as it either agreed or disagreed with his standard. While I was discoursing he would sometimes say, "Now that I like; so God has taught me." And some of his sentiments seemed very just. Yet he utterly denied the being of a devil, and declared there was no such a creature known among the Indians of old times, whose religion he supposed he was attempting to revive. He likewise told me that departed souls all went southward, and that the difference between the good and bad was this, that the former were admitted into a beautiful town with spiritual walls, or walls agreeable to the nature of souls; and that the latter would for ever hover round those walls, and in vain attempt to get in. He seemed to be sincere, honest, and conscientious in his own way and according to his own religious notions, which was more than I ever saw in any other pagan. I perceived he was looked upon, and derided amongst most of the Indians, as a precise zealot that made a needless noise about religious matters. But I must say, there was something in his temper and disposition that looked more like true religion than anything I ever observed amongst other heathen.

But alas, how deplorable is the state of the Indians upon this river! The brief representation I have here given of their notions and manners is sufficient to show that they are *led captive by Satan at his will*, in the most eminent manner. It might likewise be sufficient to excite the compassion, and engage the prayers of pious souls for these their fellow-men who sit in *the regions of the shadow of death*.

*September* 23.—Made some further attempts to instruct and Christianise the Indians on this island, but all to no purpose. They live so near the white people that they are always in the way of strong liquor, as well as the ill examples of nominal Christians; which renders it so unspeakably difficult to treat with them about Christianity.

FORKS OF DELAWARE, 1745.

*October* 1.—Discoursed to the Indians here, and spent some time in private conferences with them about their souls, and afterwards invited them to accompany, or, if not, to follow me down to Crossweeksung as soon as their conveniency would admit. Several of them cheerfully accepted the invitation.

CROSSWEEKSUNG, IN NEW JERSEY, 1745.

Preached to my people from John xiv. 1–6. The divine presence seemed to be in the assembly. Numbers were affected with divine truth, and it was a season of comfort to some in particular. What a difference is there between these and the Indians I had lately treated with upon Susquehanna! To be with *those* seemed like being banished from God and all His people; to be with *these* like being admitted into His family and to the enjoyment of His divine presence. How great is the change lately made upon numbers of these Indians, who not many months ago were as thoughtless and averse to Christianity as those upon Susquehanna; and how astonishing is that grace which has made this change!

*Lord's day, October* 6.—Preached in the forenoon from John x. 7–11. There was a considerable melting among my people; the dear young Christians were refreshed, comforted, and strengthened, and one or two persons newly awakened. In the afternoon I discoursed on the story of the jailer, Acts xvi. In the evening expounded Acts xx. 1-12. At this time a very agreeable melting spread through the whole assembly. I scarcely ever saw a more desirable affection in any number of people in my life. There was hardly a dry eye to be seen among them, and yet nothing boisterous or unseemly, nothing that tended to disturb the public worship; but rather to encourage and excite Christian ardour and a spirit of true devotion. Those who, I have reason to hope, were savingly renewed were first affected, and seemed to rejoice much, but with brokenness of spirit and godly fear. Their exercises were much the same with those mentioned in my Journal of August 26, evidently appearing to be the genuine effect of a *Spirit of adoption.*

After public service was over I withdrew (being much tired with the labours of the day), and the Indians continued praying among themselves for near two hours together; which continued exercises appeared to be attended with a blessed quickening influence from on high. I could not but earnestly wish that numbers of God's people had been present at this season, to see and hear these things which I am sure must refresh the heart of every true lover of Zion's interest. To see those who very lately were pagan idolaters, *having no hope and without God in the world*, now filled with a sense of divine love and grace, and worshipping the *Father in spirit and in truth*, as numbers here appeared to do, was not a little affecting; and especially to see them appear so tender and humble, as well as lively, fervent, and devout in the divine service.

*October* 24. — Discoursed from John iv. 13, 14. There was great attention, and an unaffected melting in the assembly. It is surprising to see how eager they are of hearing the Word of God. I have oftentimes thought they would cheerfully and diligently attend divine worship twenty-four hours together, had they an opportunity so to do.

*October* 25.—Discoursed to my people respecting the resurrection, from Luke xx. 27–36. When I came to mention the blessedness which the godly shall then enjoy, their final freedom from death, sin, and sorrow; their equality with the angels in regard to nearness and enjoyment of Christ (some imperfect degree of which they are favoured with in the present life), and their being the children of God, openly acknowledged by Him as such—when I mentioned these things, numbers of them were much affected and melted with a view of this blessed state.

*October* 26.—Being called to assist in the administration of the Lord's Supper in a neighbouring congregation, I invited my people to go with me, who in general embraced the opportunity cheerfully, and attended the several discourses of that solemnity with diligence and affection, most of them now understanding something of the English language.

*Lord's day, October* 27.—While I was preaching to a vast assembly of people abroad, who appeared generally easy and secure, there was one Indian woman, a stranger, who never heard me preach before, nor ever regarded anything about religion (being now persuaded by some of her friends to come to meeting, though much against her will), was seized with pressing concern for her soul, and soon after expressed a great desire of going home (more than forty miles distant), to call her husband, that he also might be awakened to a concern for his soul. Some other of the Indians also appeared to be affected with divine truth this day.

The pious people of the English, numbers of whom I had opportunity to converse with, seemed refreshed with seeing the Indians worship God in that devout and solemn manner with the assembly of His people. With those mentioned in Acts xi. 18, they could not but *glorify God, saying, Then hath God also to the Gentiles granted repentance unto life.*

*October* 28.—Preached again to a great assembly, and some of my people appeared affected. When public worship was over, they were inquisitive whether there would not be another sermon in the evening, or before the sacramental solemnity was concluded; being still desirous to hear God's Word.

*October* 28.—Discoursed from Matthew xxii. 1–13. I was enabled to open the Scripture, and adapt my discourse and expressions to the capacities of my people, I know not how, in a plain, easy, and familiar manner, beyond all that I could have done by the utmost study; and this, without any special difficulty, with as much freedom as if I had been addressing a common audience, who had been instructed in the doctrine of Christianity all their days.

The Word of God at this time seemed to fall upon the assembly with a divine power and influence, especially toward the close of my discourse; there was both a sweet melting and bitter mourning in the audience. Christians were refreshed and comforted, convictions were revived in others, and several persons newly awakened, who had never been with us before. So much of the divine presence appeared in the assembly, that it seemed *this was no other than the house of God and the gate of heaven.* And all that had any savour and relish of divine things were even constrained by the sweetness of that season to say, *Lord, it is good for us to be here.* If ever there was amongst my people an appearance of the New Jerusalem, *as a bride adorned for her husband,* there was much of it at this time; and so agreeable was the entertainment where such tokens of the divine presence were, that I could scarcely be willing in the evening to leave the place and repair to my lodgings. I was refreshed with a view of the continuance of this blessed work of grace among them, and its influence upon strangers of the Indians that had of late, from time to time, providentially fallen into these parts.

*November* 1.—Discoursed from Luke xxiv., briefly explaining the whole chapter, and insisting especially upon some particular passages. The discourse produced an affectionate concern in some of the hearers, though not equal to what has often appeared among them.

*Lord's day, November 3.*—Preached to my people from Luke xvi. 17, more especially for the sake of several lately brought under deep concern for their souls. There was some apparent concern and affection in the assembly, though far less than has been usual of late. Afterwards I baptized fourteen of the Indians, six adults and eight children. One of these was near fourscore years of age, and I have reason to hope God has brought her savingly home to Himself. Two of the others were men of fifty years old, who had been remarkable even among the Indians for their wickedness; one of them had been a murderer, and both notorious drunkards, as well as excessively quarrelsome; yet now I cannot but hope both are become subjects of divine grace, especially the worst of them.[1]   I deferred their baptism for many weeks after they had given evidence of having passed a great change, that I might have more opportunities to observe the fruits of those impressions they had been under, and apprehended the way was now clear.   There was not one of the adults I baptized, but what had given me some comfortable grounds to hope that God had wrought a work of special grace in their hearts, although I could not find the same satisfaction respecting one or two of them.

*November* 4.—Discoursed from John xi., briefly explaining most of the chapter.   Divine truth made deep impressions upon many in the assembly ; numbers were affected with a view of the power of Christ, manifested in His raising the dead ; and especially when this instance of His power was improved to show His power and ability to raise dead souls (such as many of them then felt themselves to be) to a spiritual life ; as also to raise the dead at the last day, and dispense to them due rewards and punishments.

Several persons lately come from remote places were now brought under deep and pressing concern for their souls ; particularly one, who not long since came half drunk, and railed on us, and attempted by all means to disturb us while engaged in worship, was now so concerned and distressed for her soul,

[1] The man particularly mentioned in my Journal of August 10th, as being then awakened.

that she seemed unable to get any ease without an interest in Christ. There were many tears and affectionate sobs and groans in the assembly in general, some weeping for themselves, others for their friends. And although persons are doubtless much easier affected now than they were in the beginning of this religious concern, when tears and cries for their souls were things unheard of among them; yet I must say their affection in general appeared genuine and unfeigned; and especially this appeared very conspicuous in those newly awakened. So that true and genuine convictions of sin seem still to be begun and promoted in many instances.

Baptized a child this day; several of the baptized persons were affected with the administration of the ordinance, being thereby reminded of their own solemn engagements. I have now baptized in all forty-seven of the Indians, twenty-three adults, and twenty-four children; thirty-five of them belonging to these parts, and the rest to the Forks of Delaware. Through grace, they have none of them as yet been left to disgrace their profession of Christianity by any scandalous or unbecoming behaviour.

I might now justly make many remarks on a work of grace so very remarkable as this has been in divers respects; but shall confine myself to a few general hints only.

(1) It is remarkable that God began this work

among the Indians at a time when I had the least hope, and to my apprehension the least rational prospect of success. My bodily strength being then much wasted by a late tedious journey to Susquehanna, where I was necessarily exposed to hardships and fatigues among the Indians; my mind being also exceedingly depressed with a view of the unsuccessfulness of my labours (since I had little reason so much as to hope that God had made me instrumental of the saving conversion of any of the Indians, except my interpreter and his wife); whence I was ready to look upon myself as a burden to the Honourable Society that employed and supported me in this business, and began to entertain serious thoughts of giving up my mission; and almost resolved I would do so at the conclusion of the present year, if I had then no better prospect of special success in my work than I had hitherto had. Yet I cannot say I entertained these thoughts because I was weary of the labours and fatigues that necessarily attended my present business, or because I had light and freedom in my own mind to turn any other way; but purely through dejection of spirit, pressing discouragement, and an apprehension of its being unjust to spend money consecrated to religious uses only to civilise the Indians and bring them to an external profession of Christianity, which was all that I could then see any prospect of having effected, while God seemed, as I thought, evidently to frown upon the design of their saving

conversion, by withholding the convincing and
renewing influences of His blessed Spirit from
attending the means I had hitherto used for that
end.

In this frame of mind I first visited these Indians
at Crossweeksung, apprehending it was my indispensable duty (seeing I had heard there was a
number in these parts) to make some attempts for
their conversion to God, though I cannot say that
I had any hopes of success, my spirits were now
so extremely sunk. And I do not know that my
hopes respecting the conversion of the Indians were
ever reduced to so low an ebb, since I had any
special concern for them, as at this time. Yet this
was the very season in which God saw fit to begin
this glorious work. Thus He *ordained strength out
of weakness,* by making bare His almighty arm at
a time when all hopes and human probabilities
appeared to fail. Whence I learn that it is good
to follow the path of duty, though in the midst of
darkness and discouragement.

(2) It is remarkable how God providentially,
and in a manner almost unaccountable, called
these Indians together to be instructed in the
great things that concerned their souls; and how
He seized their minds with the most solemn and
weighty concern for their eternal salvation as fast
as they came to the place where His Word was
preached. When I first came into these parts in
June, I found not one man at the place I visited,

but only four women and a few children; but
before I had been here many days, they gathered
from all quarters, some from more than twenty
miles distant; and when I made them a second
visit in the beginning of August, some came more
than forty miles to hear me. Many came without
any intelligence of what was going on here, and
consequently without any design of theirs, so much
as to gratify their curiosity; so that it seemed as if
God had summoned them together from all quarters
for nothing else but to deliver His message to them;
and that He did this, with regard to some of them,
without making use of any human means; although
pains were taken by some of them to give notice to
others at remote places.

Nor is it less surprising that they were one after
another affected with a solemn concern for their
souls, almost as soon as they came upon the spot
where divine truths were taught them. I often
thought that their coming to our place of worship
was like Saul and his messengers coming among
the prophets; they no sooner came but they
prophesied; and these were almost as soon affected
with a sense of their sin and misery, and with an
earnest concern for deliverance, as they made their
appearance in our assembly. After this work of
grace began with power among them, it was
common for strangers of the Indians, before they
had been with us one day, to become deeply
convinced of their sin and misery, and to enquire

with great solicitude, *What they should do to be saved.*

(3) It is likewise remarkable how God preserved these poor ignorant Indians from being prejudiced against me and the truths I taught them, by those means that were used for that purpose by ungodly people. Many attempts were made by some ill-minded persons of the white people to prejudice them against or fright them from Christianity. They sometimes told them the Indians were well enough already; that there was no need of all this noise about Christianity; that, if they were Christians, they would be in no safer or happier state than they were in already. Sometimes they told them that I was a knave, a deceiver, and the like; that I daily taught them a number of lies, and had no other design but to impose upon them.

When none of these suggestions would avail, they then tried another expedient, and told the Indians, " My design was to gather together as large a body of them as I possibly could, and then sell them to England for slaves." Nothing could be more likely to terrify the Indians than this, as they are naturally of a jealous disposition, and the most averse to a state of servitude perhaps of any people living. But all these wicked insinuations, through divine goodness overruling, constantly turned against the authors of them, and only served to engage the affections of the Indians more firmly to me. Being awakened to a solemn concern about their souls, they could not but observe that the persons who endeavoured to embitter their minds against me were altogether thoughtless, vicious, and profane ; and therefore that, if they had no concern for their own souls, it was not likely they should have any for the souls of others.

It seems yet the more wonderful that the Indians were preserved from once hearkening to these suggestions inasmuch as I was an utter stranger among them, and could give them no assurance of my sincere affection to and concern for them by anything that was past ; while the persons that insinuated these things were their old acquaintance, who had had frequent opportunities of gratifying their thirsty appetites with strong drink, and consequently had the greatest interest in their affections.   But from this instance of their preservation from fatal prejudices, I have had occasion with admiration to say, " If God will work, who can hinder or resist ? "

(4) Nor is it less wonderful how God was pleased to provide a remedy for my want of skill and freedom in the Indian language, by remarkably fitting my interpreter for and assisting him in the performance of his work. It might reasonably be supposed that I must labour under great disadvantage in addressing the Indians by an interpreter ; and that divine truths would unavoidably lose much of the energy and pathos

with which they might at first be delivered, as coming to the audience second hand. But though, to my sorrow and discouragement, this has often been the case in times past, when my interpreter had little or no sense of divine things, yet now it was quite otherwise. I cannot think my addresses to the Indians ordinarily, since the beginning of this season of grace, have lost anything of the power or pungency with which they were made, unless it were sometimes for want of pertinent and pathetic terms and expressions in the Indian language; and this difficulty could scarcely have been obviated by my personal acquaintance with the language. My interpreter had before gained some good degree of doctrinal knowledge, whereby he was rendered capable of understanding and communicating, without mistakes, the intent and meaning of my discourses, and that without being obliged to interpret *verbatim*. He had likewise an experimental acquaintance with divine things; and it pleased God at this season to inspire his mind with longing desires for the conversion of the Indians, and to give him admirable zeal and fervency in addressing them. And it is remarkable that, when I was favoured with special assistance in any work, and enabled to speak with more than common fervency and power, under a lively and affecting sense of divine things, he was usually affected in the same manner almost instantly, and seemed at once quickened and enabled to speak in the same pathetic language, and under the same influence that I did. A surprising energy often accompanied the Word at such seasons ; the face of the whole assembly would be apparently changed almost in an instant, and tears and sobs became common among them.

He also appeared to have such a clear doctrinal view of God's usual methods of dealing with souls under a preparatory work of conviction and humiliation as he never had before ; so that I could, with his help, discourse freely with the distressed persons about their internal exercises, their fears, discouragements, and temptations. He likewise took pains day and night to repeat and inculcate upon the minds of the Indians the truths I taught them daily; and this he appeared to do, not from spiritual pride and an affectation of setting himself up as a public teacher, but from a spirit of faithfulness and an honest concern for their souls.

His conversation among the Indians has likewise been savoury, such as becomes a Christian and a person employed in his work ; and I may justly say he has been a great comfort to me, and a great instrument of promoting this good work among the Indians. Whatever be the state of his own soul, it is apparent that God has remarkably fitted him for this work, and made it manifest that, without bestowing on me the gift of tongues,

He could find a way to enable me as effectually to convey the truths of His glorious Gospel to the minds of these poor benighted pagans.

(5) It is further remarkable that God has carried on His work here by such means, and in such a manner, as tended to obviate and leave no room for those prejudices and objections that have often been raised against such a work. When persons have been awakened to a solemn concern for their souls, by hearing the more awful truths of God's Word and the terrors of the divine law insisted upon, it has usually in such cases been objected by some that such persons were only frightened with a fearful noise of hell and damnation, and that there was no evidence that their concern was the effect of a divine influence. But God has left no room for this objection in the present case, this work of grace having been begun and carried on by almost one continued strain of Gospel invitation to perishing sinners, as may reasonably be guessed from a view of the passages of Scripture which I chiefly insisted upon in my discourses from time to time ; and which I have for that purpose inserted in my Journal.

Nor have I ever seen so general an awakening in any assembly in my life as appeared here, while I was opening and insisting upon the Parable of the Great Supper, Luke xiv. In which discourse I was enabled to set before my hearers the unsearchable riches of Gospel grace. Not that I would be understood here, that I never instructed the Indians respecting their fallen state and the sinfulness and misery of it; for this was what I at first chiefly insisted upon, and endeavoured to repeat and inculcate in almost every discourse, knowing that without this foundation I should but build upon the sand; and that it would be in vain to invite them to Christ, unless I could convince them of their need of Him. Yet this great awakening, this surprising concern, was never excited by any harangues of terror, but always appeared most remarkable when I insisted upon the compassion of a dying Saviour, the plentiful provisions of the Gospel, and the free offers of divine grace to needy distressed sinners. Nor would I be understood to insinuate that such a religious concern might justly be suspected as not being genuine and from a divine influence, because produced by the preaching of terror; for this is perhaps God's more usual way of awakening sinners, and appears entirely agreeable to Scripture and sound reason. But what I mean here to observe is that God saw fit to improve and bless milder means for the effectual awakening of these Indians, and thereby obviated the forementioned objection, which the world might otherwise have had a more plausible colour of making.

And as there has been no room for any plausible objection against this work in regard to the means, so neither in regard to the manner in which it has been carried on. It is true that persons' concern for their souls has been exceeding great, the convictions of their sin and misery have risen to a high degree, and produced many tears and groans; but they have not been attended with those disorders, either bodily or mental, that have sometimes prevailed among persons under religious impressions. There has been no appearance of those convulsions, bodily agonies, frightful screamings and swoonings, that have been so much complained of in some places; although there have been some who, with the jailer, have been made to tremble under a sense of their sin and misery; numbers who have been made to cry out from a distressing view of their perishing state, and some that have for a time been in great measure deprived of their bodily strength, yet without any such convulsive appearances.

Nor has there been anything of mental disorder here, such as visions, trances, imaginations of being under prophetic inspiration, and the like; or scarcely any unbecoming disposition to appear remarkably affected either with concern or joy. Yet I must confess that I observed one or two persons, whose concern I thought was in a considerable measure affected; and one whose joy appeared to be of the same kind. But these workings of spiritual pride I endeavoured to crush in the first appearances, and have not since observed any affection, either of joy or sorrow, but what appeared genuine and unaffected. But,

(6) The effects of this work have likewise been very remarkable. I doubt not but that many of these people have gained more doctrinal knowledge of divine truth, since I first visited them in June last, than could have been instilled into their minds by the most diligent use of proper and instructive means for whole years together, without such a divine influence. Their pagan notions and idolatrous practices seem to be entirely abandoned in these parts. They are regulated, and appear regularly disposed in the affairs of marriage; an instance whereof I have given in my Journal of August 14. They seem generally divorced from drunkenness, their darling vice and the *sin that easily besets them*; so that I do not know of more than two or three who have been my steady hearers, that have drunk to excess since I first visited them, although it was common before for some or other of them to be drunk almost every day; and some of them seem now to fear this sin in particular more than death itself. A principle of honesty and justice appears in many of them, they are concerned to discharge their old debts, which they have neglected and perhaps scarcely thought of for years past. Their manner of living is much more decent and comfortable than formerly, having now the benefit of that money which they used to consume upon

strong drink. Love seems to reign among them, especially those who have given evidences of a saving change; and I never saw any appearance of bitterness or censoriousness in these, nor any disposition to esteem themselves better than others, who had not received the like mercy.

As their sorrows under conviction have been great and pressing, so many of them have since appeared to *rejoice with joy unspeakable and full of glory*; yet I never saw anything ecstatic or flighty in their joy. Their consolations do not incline them to lightness; on the contrary, they are attended with solemnity, oftentimes with tears, and an apparent brokenness of heart, as may be seen in several passages of my Journal. In this respect some of them have been surprised at themselves, and have with concern observed to me that, " when their hearts have been glad " (which is a phrase they commonly make use of to express spiritual joy), " they could not help crying for all."

Upon the whole, I think I may justly say, here are all the symptoms and evidences of a remarkable work of grace among these Indians that can reasonably be desired or expected. May the great Author of this work maintain and promote the same here, and propagate it everywhere, till *the whole earth be filled with His glory*! Amen.

I have now rode more than three thousand miles, that I have kept an exact account of, since the beginning of March last; and almost the whole of it has been in my own proper business as a missionary, upon the design, either immediately or more remotely, of propagating Christian knowledge among the Indians. I have taken pains to look out for a colleague or companion to travel with me; and have likewise used endeavours to procure something for his support among religious persons in New England, which cost me a journey of several hundred miles in length; but have not as yet found any person qualified and disposed for this good work, although I had some encouragement from ministers and others, that it was hopeful a maintenance might be procured for one, when the man should be found.

I have likewise of late represented to the gentlemen concerned with the mission the necessity of having an English school speedily set up among these Indians, who are now willing to be at the pains of gathering together in a body for this purpose. And, in order to it, I have humbly proposed to them the collecting of money for the maintenance of a schoolmaster, and defraying of other necessary charges in the promotion of this good work; which they are now attempting in the various congregations of Christians to which they respectively belong.

The several companies of Indians I have preached to in the summer past live at great distances from each other. It is more than seventy miles from Crossweeksung in New Jersey to the Forks of

Delaware in Pennsylvania; and from thence to
sundry of the Indian settlements I visited on
Susquehanna, it is more than a hundred and
twenty miles. And so much of my time is
necessarily consumed in journeying, that I can
have but little for any of my necessary studies, and
consequently for the study of the Indian languages
in particular; especially as I am obliged to discourse so frequently to the Indians at each of these
places while I am with them, in order to redeem
time to visit the rest. I am at times almost
discouraged from attempting to gain any acquaintance with the Indian languages, they are so very
numerous, and especially seeing my other labours
and fatigues engross almost the whole of my time,
and bear exceeding hard upon my constitution,
so that my health is much impaired. However, I
have taken considerable pains to learn the Delaware
language, and propose still to do so, as far as my
other business and bodily health will admit. I
have already made some proficiency in it, though
I have laboured under great disadvantages in my
attempts of that nature. And it is but just to
observe here that all the pains I took to acquaint
myself with the language of the Indians with
whom I spent my first year, were of little or no
service to me here among the Delawares; so that
my work, when I came among these Indians was
all to begin anew.

As these poor ignorant pagans stood in need of

having *line upon line and precept upon precept*, in order to their being instructed and grounded in the principles of Christianity; so I preached *publicly, and taught from house to house,* almost every day for whole weeks together, when I was with them. And my public discourses did not then make up one half of my work, while so many were constantly coming up to me with that important enquiry, *What must we do to be saved?* and opening to me the various exercises of their minds. Yet I can say, to the praise of rich grace, that the apparent success with which my labours were crowned unspeakably more than compensated for the labour itself, and was likewise a great means of supporting and carrying me through the business and fatigues, which it seems my nature would have sunk under without such an encouraging prospect. But although this success has afforded matter of support, comfort, and thankfulness; yet in this season I have found great need of assistance in my work, and have been much oppressed for want of one to bear a part of my labours and hardships.

May the Lord of the harvest send forth other labourers into this part of His harvest, that those who sit in darkness may see great light, and that the whole earth may be filled with the knowledge of Himself! Amen.

DAVID BRAINERD.

*November* 20, 1745.

## PART II.

### DIVINE GRACE DISPLAYED; OR, THE CONTINUANCE AND PROGRESS OF A REMARKABLE WORK OF GRACE AMONG THE INDIANS.

CROSSWEEKSUNG, IN NEW JERSEY, 1745.

*Lord's day, November 24.* — Preached both parts of the day from the story of Zacchæus, Luke xix. 1–9. In the latter exercise, when I opened and insisted upon the salvation that comes to the sinner, upon his becoming a son of Abraham or a true believer, the Word seemed to be attended with divine power to the hearts of the hearers. Numbers were much affected, former convictions were revived, one or two persons newly awakened, and a most affectionate engagement in divine service appeared among them universally.

These impressions appeared to be the genuine effect of God's Word brought home to their hearts, by the power and influence of the divine Spirit.

*November 26.* — After spending some time in private conferences with my people, I discoursed publicly among them from John v. 1–9. I was favoured with some special freedom and fervency in my discourse, and a powerful energy accompanied the Word. Many wept, and scarcely any appeared unconcerned in the whole assembly. The influence that seized the audience appeared gentle, and yet pungent and efficacious. It produced no boisterous commotion of the passions, but seemed deeply to affect the heart; and excited in the persons under conviction of their lost state heavy groans and tears; and in others who had obtained comfort a sweet and humble melting. It seemed like the gentle but steady showers that effectually water the earth, without violently beating upon the surface.

The persons lately awakened were deeply distressed for their souls, and appeared earnestly solicitous to obtain an interest in Christ; and some of them, after public worship was over, in anguish of spirit said, "They knew not what to do, nor how to get their wicked hearts changed."

*November* 28.—Discoursed to the Indians publicly, after having privately endeavoured to instruct some of them in the duties of Christianity. Opened and made remarks upon the sacred story of our Lord's transfiguration, Luke ix. 28–36, principally with a view to the edification and consolation of God's people. I observed some who, I have reason to think, are truly such, exceedingly affected with an account of the glory of Christ in His transfiguration, and filled with longing desires of being with Him that they might with open face behold His glory.

After public service was over, I asked one of them who wept much what she wanted. She replied, "O to be with Christ! She did not know how to stay." This was a blessed refreshing season to the religious people in general. The Lord Jesus Christ seemed to manifest His divine glory to them, as when transfigured before His disciples; and they, with the disciples, were ready universally to say, *Lord, it is good to be here.*

The influence of God's Word was not confined to those who had given evidences of being truly gracious, though at this time my discourse was directed chiefly to such; but it appeared to be a season of divine power in the whole assembly, so that most were in some measure affected. One aged man in particular, lately awakened, was now brought under deep and pressing concern for his soul, and was earnestly inquisitive "how he might find Jesus Christ." God seems still to vouchsafe His divine presence and the influence of His blessed Spirit to accompany His Word, at least in some measure, in all our meetings for divine worship.

*November 30.*—Preached near night, after having spent some hours in private conference with some of my people about their souls. Explained and insisted upon the story of the rich man and Lazarus, Luke xvi. 19–26. The Word made powerful impressions upon many in the assembly, especially while I discoursed of the blessedness of Lazarus in Abraham's bosom. This I could perceive affected them much more than what I spoke of the rich man's misery and torments. Thus it has been usually with them; they have appeared more affected with the comfortable than the dreadful truths of God's Word. That which has distressed many of them under conviction is, that they found they wanted and could not obtain the happiness of the godly; at least they have often appeared to be more affected with this than with the terrors of hell. But whatever be the means of their awakening, it is plain numbers are made deeply sensible of their sin and misery, the wickedness and stubbornness of their own hearts, their utter inability to help themselves or to come to Christ for help without divine assistance, and so are brought to see their perishing need of Christ to do all for them, and to lie at the foot of sovereign mercy.

*Lord's day, December* 1. — Discoursed to my people in the forenoon from Luke xvi. 27, 31. There appeared an unfeigned affection in divers persons, and some seemed deeply impressed with divine truths. In the afternoon preached to a number of white people; at which time the Indians attended with diligence, and many of them were able to understand a considerable part of the discourse. At night discoursed to my people again, and gave them some particular cautions relating to their conduct. I pressed them to watchfulness in all their deportment, seeing they were encompassed with those that waited for their halting, and who stood ready to draw them into temptations of every kind, and then to expose religion on their account.

*Lord's day, December* 8. — Discoursed on the story of the blind man, John ix. There appeared no remarkable effect of the Word upon the assembly at this time. Those who have lately been much concerned for their souls, seemed now not so affected nor solicitous to obtain an interest in Christ as has been usual, although they attended with seriousness and diligence. Such have been the doings of the Lord here in awakening sinners, and affecting the hearts of those who are brought to solid comfort with a fresh sense of divine things from time to time, that it is now strange to see the assembly sit with dry eyes, and without sobs and groans.

*December* 12.—Preached from the Parable of the Ten Virgins, Matthew xxv. The divine power seemed in some measure to attend this discourse, in which I was favoured with uncommon freedom and plainness of address, and enabled to open and explain divine truths to the capacities of my people in a manner beyond myself. There appeared in many persons an affectionate concern for their souls; although the concern in general seemed not so deep and pressing as formerly. Yet it was refreshing to see many melted into tears and unaffected sobs; some with a sense of divine love, and some for want of it.

*Lord's day, December* 15. — Preached to the

Indians from Luke xiii. 24–28.    Divine truths fell
with weight and power upon the audience, and
seemed to reach the hearts of many.    Near night
discoursed to them again from Matthew xxv. 31–46.
At this season also the Word appeared to be accompanied with a divine influence, and made powerful
impressions upon the assembly in general, as well
as upon divers persons more especially.    This
was an amazing season of grace.    The Word
of the Lord was *quick and powerful, sharper than a
two-edged sword, and pierced to the hearts* of many.
The assembly was greatly affected and deeply
wrought upon, yet without so much apparent
commotion of the passions as was usual in the
beginning of this work of grace.    The impressions
made upon the audience appeared solid and rational,
worthy of the solemn truths by means of which
they were produced, and far from being the effects
of any sudden fright or groundless perturbation of
mind.    The hearts of the hearers seemed to bow
under the weight of divine truth, and how evident
did it now appear that they received it *not as the
word of man but as the Word of God.*    None can
frame a just idea of the appearance of our assembly
at this time, but those who have seen a congregation solemnly awed and deeply impressed by the
special power and influence of truth delivered to
them in the name of the Lord.

*December* 16.—Discoursed to my people in the
evening from Luke xi. 1–13.    After having insisted

some time upon the ninth verse, wherein there is a command and encouragement to ask for divine favours, I called upon them to ask for a new heart with the utmost importunity, as the man mentioned in the parable pleaded for loaves of bread at midnight. There was much affection and concern in the assembly; one woman especially appeared in great distress. She was brought to such an agony in seeking after Christ, that the sweat ran off her face for a considerable time together, although the evening was very cold, and her bitter cries were the most affecting indication of the inward anguish of her heart.

*December* 21.—My people having now attained to a considerable degree of knowledge in the principles of Christianity, I thought it proper to set up a Catechetical Lecture among them. This evening I attempted something in that form; proposing questions to them agreeable to the Assembly's Shorter Catechism, receiving their answers, and then explaining and enforcing each question as it might appear necessary. After this I endeavoured to make some practical improvement of the whole. They were able readily and rationally to answer many important questions I proposed to them; so that I found their doctrinal knowledge to exceed my own expectations. In the improvement of my discourse, when I came to explain the blessedness of those who have so great and glorious a God for their everlasting Friend and

Portion, several of my hearers were much affected; especially, when I exhorted and endeavoured to persuade them to be reconciled to God through His dear Son, and thus to secure an interest in His everlasting favour. They appeared to be not only enlightened and instructed, but affected and engaged in their souls' concern by this method of discoursing.

*Lord's day, December 22.*—Discoursed upon the story of the young man in the Gospel, Matthew xix. 16–22. God made it a seasonable word, I am persuaded, to some souls. Several of the Indians newly come here had frequently lived among Quakers; and being more civilised and conformed to English manners than the generality of the Indians, they had imbibed some of the Quakers' errors, especially this fundamental one, That if men will but live soberly and honestly, according to the dictates of their own consciences, or the light within, there is then no danger or doubt of their salvation. I found these persons much worse to deal with than those who are wholly under pagan darkness, who make no pretences to knowledge in Christianity at all, nor have any self-righteous foundation to stand upon. However they all, except one, appeared now convinced that this sober honest life of itself was not sufficient to salvation; since Christ Himself had declared it so in the case of the young ruler. They seemed in some measure concerned to obtain that change of heart which I had been labouring to show them the necessity of.

This was likewise a season of comfort to some souls, and in particular to one (the same mentioned in my Journal of the 16th inst.) who never before obtained any settled comfort, though I have abundant reason to think she had experienced a saving change some days before. She now appeared in a heavenly frame of mind, composed and delighted with the divine will. When I came to discourse particularly with her, and enquire how she got relief and deliverance from the spiritual distresses she had lately been under, she answered in broken English, " Me try, me try, save myself, last my strength be all gone (meaning her ability to save herself), could not me stir bit farther. Den last me forced let Jesus Christ alone, send me hell if He please." [1] I said, But you were not willing to go to hell, were you? She replied, " Could not me help it. My heart he would wicked for all. Could not me make him good." [2] I asked her how she got out of this case. She answered still in the same broken language. " By

[1] In proper English thus: " I tried and tried to save myself, till at last my strength was all gone, and I could not stir any farther. Then at last I was forced to let Jesus Christ alone to send me to hell if He pleased."

[2] In plain English thus: " I could not help it. My heart would be wicked for all that I could do. I could not make it good."

by, my heart be grad desperately." I asked her why her heart was glad. She replied, "Grad my heart Jesus Christ do what He please with me. Den me tink, grad my heart Jesus Christ send me hell. Did not me care where He put me, me lobe Him for all." [1] She could not readily be convinced, but that she was willing to go to hell if Christ was pleased to send her there. Though the truth evidently was, her will was so swallowed up in the divine will, that she could not frame any hell in her imagination that would be dreadful or undesirable, provided it was but the will of God to send her to it.

Toward night discoursed to them again in the Catechetical method, which I entered upon the evening before. And when I came to improve the truths I had explained to them, and to answer that question, " But how shall I know whether God has chosen me to everlasting life ? " by pressing them to come and give up their hearts to Christ, and thereby to make their election sure ; they then appeared much affected. The persons under concern were afresh engaged in seeking after an interest in Him ; while some others, who had obtained comfort before, were refreshed to find

---

[1] " By and by my heart was exceeding glad—My heart was glad that Jesus Christ would do with me what He pleased. Then I thought my heart would be glad although Christ should send me to hell. I did not care where He put me, I should love Him for all, *i.e.* do what He would do with me."

that love to God in themselves, which was an evidence of His electing love to them.

*December 25.*—The Indians having been used upon Christmas-days to drink and revel among some of the white people in these parts, I thought it proper this day to call them together, and discourse to them upon divine things; which I accordingly did from the Parable of the Barren Fig-tree, Luke xiii. 6–9. A divine influence evidently accompanied the Word at this season. The power of God appeared in the assembly, not by producing any remarkable cries, but by breaking and melting the hearts of several who were scarce ever moved with any concern before. The power attending divine truth resembled the earthquake, rather than the whirlwind. Their passions were not so much alarmed as has been common here in times past, but their judgments appeared to be powerfully convinced by the conquering influence of divine truth. The impressions made upon the assembly in general seemed not superficial, but deep and heart-affecting. O how ready did they now appear universally to embrace and comply with everything they heard and were convinced was duty! God was in the midst of us of a truth, bowing and melting stubborn hearts. How many tears and sobs were then to be seen and heard among us! What liveliness and strict attention! what eagerness and intenseness of mind appeared in the whole assembly in the time of divine service!

They seemed to watch and wait for the dropping of God's Word, as the thirsty earth for the former and latter rain.

Afterwards I discoursed to them on the duty of husbands and wives, from Ephesians v. 22–33; and have reason to think this was a word in season. Spent some time further in the evening in inculcating the truths I had insisted upon in my former discourse respecting the barren fig-tree, and observed a powerful influence still accompany what was spoken.

*December 26.*—This evening I was visited by a person under great spiritual exercise, the most remarkable instance of this kind I ever saw. It was a woman of more than fourscore, who appeared to be so much broken and childish through age that it seemed impossible to instil into her mind any notions of divine things, or so much as to give her any doctrinal instruction, for she seemed incapable of being taught. She was led by the hand into my house, and appeared in extreme anguish. I asked her what ailed her. She answered, "That her heart was distressed, and she feared she should never find Christ." I asked her several questions relating to her distress. To all which she answered, for substance, to this effect, That she had heard me preach many times, but never knew anything about it, never "felt in her heart" till the last Sabbath; then it came, she said, "all one as if a needle had been thrust into her heart"; since which time she had no rest day nor night. She added that, on the evening before Christmas, a number of Indians being together at the house where she was, and discoursing about Christ, their talk pierced her heart so that she could not sit up, but fell down on her bed; at which time "she went away," as she expressed it, and felt as if she dreamed, and yet is confident she did not dream. When she was thus gone, she saw two paths, one appeared very broad and crooked; and that, she says, turned to the left hand. The other appeared straight and very narrow; and that went up the hill to the right hand. She travelled, she said, for some time up the narrow right-hand path, till at length something seemed to obstruct her journey. She sometimes called it darkness, and then described it otherwise, and seemed to compare it to a block or bar. She then remembered what she had heard me say about *striving to enter in at the strait gate* (although she took little notice of it at the time when she heard me discourse upon that subject), and thought she would climb over this bar. But just as she was thinking of this, she came back again, as she termed it, meaning that she came to herself; whereupon her soul was extremely distressed, apprehending she had now turned back and forsaken Christ, and that there was therefore no hope of mercy for her.

As I was sensible that trances and imaginary

views of things are of dangerous tendency in religion when sought after and depended upon; so I could not but be much concerned about this exercise, especially at first; apprehending this might be a design of Satan to bring a blemish upon the work of God here by introducing visionary scenes, imaginary terrors, and all manner of mental disorders and delusions, in the room of genuine convictions of sin and the enlightening influences of the blessed Spirit. I was almost resolved to declare that I looked upon this to be one of Satan's devices, and to caution my people against it, and the like exercises, as such. However, I determined first to enquire into her knowledge, to see whether she had any just views of things that might be the occasion of her present distress, or whether it was a mere fright arising only from imaginary terrors. I asked her several questions respecting man's primitive and present state, and respecting her own heart; which she answered rationally and to my surprise. I thought it next to impossible, if not altogether so, that a pagan who was become a child through age should in that state gain so much knowledge by any mere human instruction, without being remarkably enlightened by a divine influence.

I then proposed to her the provision made in the Gospel for the salvation of sinners, and the ability and willingness of Christ to save to the uttermost all, old as well as young, that come to

Him. To this she seemed to give a hearty assent. But instantly replied, " Ay, but I cannot come; my wicked heart will not come to Christ; I do not know how to come." She spoke this in anguish of spirit, striking on her breast, with tears in her eyes, and with such earnestness in her looks as was indeed piteous and affecting. She seems to be really convinced of her sin and misery, and her need of a change of heart; and her concern is abiding and constant. Nothing appears but that this exercise may have a saving issue; she is so solicitous to obtain an interest in Christ that her heart, as she expresses it, prays day and night.

How far God may make use of the imagination in awakening some persons under these and such like circumstances, I cannot pretend to determine; and whether this exercise I have mentioned be from a divine influence, I shall leave others to judge. But this I must say that its effects hitherto bespeak it to be such; nor can it as I see be accounted for in a rational way, but from the influence of some spirit, either good or evil. The woman I am sure never heard divine things treated of in the manner she now viewed them; and it would seem strange she should get such a rational notion of them from the mere working of her own fancy, without some superior or foreign aid. Yet I must say, I have looked upon it as one of the glories of this work of grace among the Indians, and a special evidence of its being from a divine influence, that there has till now been no appearance of such things, no visionary notions, trances, and imaginations, intermixed with those rational convictions of sin and solid consolations, which numbers have experienced. And might I have had my desire, there had been no appearance of anything of this nature at all.

*December* 28.—Discoursed to my people in the Catechetical method I lately entered upon. During the improvement of my discourse, wherein I was comparing man's present with his primitive state, showing what he had fallen from, the miseries to which he is now exposed, and pressing sinners to take a view of their deplorable circumstances without Christ, also to strive that they might obtain an interest in Him; the Lord, I trust, granted a remarkable influence of His blessed Spirit to accompany what was spoken, and a great concern appeared in the assembly. Many were melted into tears, and the impressions made upon them seemed deep and heart-affecting. In particular, there were two or three persons who appeared to be brought to the last exercises of a preparatory work, and reduced almost to extremity; being in a great measure convinced of the impossibility of helping themselves, or of mending their own hearts; and seemed to be upon the point of giving up all hope in themselves, and of venturing upon Christ as helpless and undone. Yet they were in distress and anguish because they saw no safety in so doing, unless they could do something towards saving themselves. One of these persons was the very aged woman above mentioned, who now appeared *weary and heavy laden* with a sense of her sin and misery, and her perishing need of an interest in Christ.

*Lord's day, December 29.*—Preached from John iii. 1–5. A number of white people were present, as is usual upon the Sabbath. The discourse was accompanied with power, and seemed to have a silent but deep and piercing influence upon the audience. Many wept affectionately, and there were some tears among the white people as well as the Indians. Some could not refrain from crying out, though there were not many so exercised. The impressions made upon their hearts appeared chiefly by the extraordinary earnestness of their attention, and their heavy sighs and tears.

After public worship was over, I went to my house, proposing to preach again after a short season of intermission. But they soon came in one after another, with tears in their eyes, to know what they should do to be saved. And the divine Spirit in such a manner set home upon their hearts what I spoke to them, that the house was soon filled with cries and groans. They all flocked together upon this occasion, and those whom I had reason to think in a Christless state were almost universally seized with concern about their souls. It was a season of great power among them; it seemed as if God had *bowed the heavens and come down.* So astonishingly prevalent was the operation upon old as well as young, that it seemed as if none would be left in a state of carnal security, but that God was now about to convert all the world. And I was ready to think then that I should never again despair of the conversion of any man or woman living, be they who or what they would.

It is impossible to give a just and lively description of the appearance of things at this season, at least such as to convey a bright and adequate idea of the effects of this influence. A number might now be seen rejoicing, that God had not taken away the powerful influence of His blessed Spirit from this place. It was refreshing to see so many *striving to enter in at the strait gate,* and others animated with such concern for them that they wanted "to push them forward," as some of them expressed it. At the same time numbers both of men and women, old and young, might be seen in tears, and some in anguish of spirit, appearing in their very countenances, like condemned malefactors bound towards the place of execution, with a heavy solicitude sitting in their faces; so that there seemed here, as I thought, a lively emblem of the solemn day of accounts; a mixture of heaven and hell, of joy unspeakable and anguish inexpressible.

The concern and religious affection was such that I could not pretend to have any formal religious exercise among them; but spent the time in discoursing to one and another, as I thought most proper and seasonable, and sometimes addressed them together, and finally concluded with prayer. Such were their circumstances at this season that I could scarcely have half-an-hour's rest from speaking, from about half an hour before twelve o'clock, at which time I began public worship, till past seven at night. There appeared to be four or five persons newly awakened this day and the evening before, some of whom but very lately came among us.

*December 30.*—Was visited by four or five young persons, who were lately awakened. They wept much while I discoursed to them, and endeavoured to press upon them the necessity of flying to Christ for salvation, without delay.

*December 31.*—Spent some hours this day in visiting my people from house to house, and conversing with them about their spiritual concerns; endeavouring to press upon Christless souls the necessity of a renovation of heart. I scarcely left a house, without leaving some or other of its inhabitants in tears, appearing solicitously engaged to obtain an interest in Christ. The Indians are now gathered together from all quarters to this place, and have built them little cottages, so that more than twenty families live within a quarter of a mile of me ; a very convenient situation in regard both of public and private instruction.

*January* 1, 1745-6. — Spent some considerable time in visiting my people again. Found scarce one but what was under serious impressions respecting their spiritual concerns.

*January* 2.—Visited some persons newly come among us, who had scarce ever heard anything of Christianity, except the empty name, before. Endeavoured to instruct them particularly in the first principles of religion, in the most easy and familiar manner I could. Strangers from remote parts are almost continually dropping in among us, so that I have occasion repeatedly to open and inculcate the first principles of Christianity.

*January* 4.—Prosecuted my Catechetical method of instructing. Found my people able to answer questions with propriety, beyond what could have been expected from persons so lately brought out of heathen darkness. In the improvement of my discourse, there appeared some concern and affection in the assembly ; and especially those of whom I entertained hopes as being truly gracious, at least several of them were much affected and refreshed.

*Lord's day, January* 5.—Discoursed from Matthew xii. 10–13. There appeared not so much liveliness and affection in divine service as usual. The same truths that have often produced many tears in the assembly, seemed now to have no special influence upon any.

Near night I proposed to proceed in my usual method of catechising, but, while we were engaged in the first prayer, the power of God seemed to descend upon the assembly in such a remarkable manner, and so many appeared under pressing concern for their souls, that I thought it much more expedient to insist upon the plentiful provision made by divine grace for the redemption of perishing sinners, and to press them to a speedy acceptance of the great salvation, than to ask them questions about doctrinal points. What was most practical seemed most seasonable to be insisted upon, while numbers appeared so extraordinarily solicitous to obtain an interest in the great Redeemer.

Baptized two persons this day; one adult, the woman particularly mentioned in my Journal of December 22, and one child. This woman has discovered a sweet and heavenly frame of mind from time to time, since her first reception of comfort. One morning in particular she came to see me, discovering an unusual joy and satisfaction in her countenance; and when I enquired into the reason of it, she replied, "That God had made her feel that it was right for Him to do what He pleased with all things; and that it would be right if He should cast her husband and son both into hell," though it was apparent she loved them dearly. She moreover enquired whether I was not sent to preach to the Indians by some good people

a great way off.   I replied, Yes, by the good people
in Scotland.   She answered that her heart loved
those good people so, the evening before, that she
could scarce help praying for them all night; her
heart would go to God for them.   Thus the blessing of such as are ready to perish is likely to come
upon those pious persons who have communicated
of their substance to the propagation of the Gospel.

*January* 11.—Discoursed in a Catechetical method,
as usual of late.   Having opened our first parent's
apostasy from God and our fall in him, I proceeded to improve my discourse, by showing the
necessity of an almighty Redeemer, and the absolute
need every sinner has of an interest in His merits
and mediation.   Some tenderness and affectionate
concern appeared in the assembly.

*Lord's day, January* 12.—Preached from Isaiah
lv. 6.   The Word of God seemed to fall upon the
audience with a divine weight and influence, and
evidently appeared to be *not the word of man.*   The
blessed Spirit, I am persuaded, accompanied what
was spoken to the hearts of many; and there was
a powerful revival of conviction in numbers who
were under spiritual exercise before.

Toward night, catechised in my usual method.
Near the close of my discourse, there appeared a
great concern and much affection in the audience,
which increased while I continued to invite them
to come to an all-sufficient Redeemer for eternal
salvation.   The Spirit of God seems, from time to

time, to be striving with numbers of souls here. They are so frequently and repeatedly roused that they seem unable at present to lull themselves asleep.

*January* 13. — Was visited by several persons under deep concern, one of whom was newly awakened. It is a most agreeable work to treat with souls who are solicitously enquiring what they shall do to be saved; and as we are never to be *weary in well doing,* so the obligation seems to be peculiarly strong when the work is so very desirable. Yet I must say my health is so much impaired, and my spirits so wasted with my labours and solitary manner of living (there being no human creature in the house with me), that their repeated and almost incessant applications to me for help and direction are sometimes exceeding burdensome, and so exhaust my spirits that I become fit for nothing at all, entirely unable to prosecute any business sometimes for days together. And what contributes much toward this difficulty is, that I am obliged to spend much time in communicating a little matter to them; there being oftentimes many things necessary to be premised, before I can speak directly to what I principally aim at; which things would readily be taken for granted where there was a competency of doctrinal knowledge.

*January* 14.—Spent some time in private conferences with my people, and found some disposed to take comfort, as I thought, upon slight grounds.

They are now generally awakened, and it is become so disgraceful, as well as terrifying to the conscience, to be destitute of religion, that they are in imminent danger of taking up with any appearances of grace, rather than to live under the fear and disgrace of an unregenerate state.

*January* 18.—Prosecuted my Catechetical method of discoursing. There appeared a great solemnity, and some considerable affection in the assembly. I find this method of instructing very profitable. When I first entered upon it, I was exercised with fears, lest my discourses would unavoidably be so doctrinal that they would tend only to enlighten the head, but not to affect the heart. But the event proves quite otherwise; for these exercises have hitherto been remarkably blessed in the latter as well as the former respect.

*Lord's day, January* 19.—Discoursed to my people from Isaiah lv. 7. Towards night catechised in my ordinary method. This appeared to be a powerful season of grace among us; numbers were much affected; convictions powerfully revived, and believers in general were refreshed and strengthened. One weary heavy-laden soul, I have abundant reason to hope, was brought to true rest and solid comfort in Christ, who afterwards gave me such an account of God's dealings with him as was abundantly satisfying as well as refreshing to me.

He told me, he had often heard me say that persons must see and feel themselves utterly helpless and undone; that they must be emptied of a dependence upon themselves, and of all hope of saving themselves by their own doings, in order to their coming to Christ for salvation. He had long been striving after this view of things, supposing this would be an excellent frame of mind to be thus emptied of a dependence upon his own goodness; that God would have respect to this frame, would then be well pleased with him, and bestow eternal life upon him. But when he came to feel himself in this helpless undone condition, he found it quite contrary to all his thoughts and expectations; so that it was not the same, nor indeed anything like the frame he had been seeking after. Instead of its being a good frame of mind, he now found nothing but badness in himself, and saw it was for ever impossible for him to make himself any better. He wondered, he said, that he had ever hoped to mend his own heart. He was amazed he had never before seen that it was utterly impossible for him, by all his contrivances and endeavours, to do anything that way, since the matter now appeared to him in so clear a light. Instead of imagining now that God would be pleased with him for the sake of this frame of mind, and this view of his undone state, he saw clearly and felt it would be just with God to send him to eternal misery, and that there was no goodness in what he then felt; for he could not help seeing that he was naked, sinful and miserable, and there was nothing in such a sight to deserve God's love or pity. He saw these things in a manner so clear and convincing, that it seemed to him, he said, he could convince everybody of their utter inability ever to help themselves, and their un-worthiness of any help from God.

In this frame of mind he came to public worship this evening; and while I was inviting sinners to come to Christ, without any goodness of their own to recommend them, he thought with himself that he had often tried to come and give up his heart to Christ, and he used to hope that some time or other he should be able to do so. But now he was convinced he could not, and it seemed utterly vain for him ever to try any more; and he could not, he said, find a heart to make any further attempt, because he saw it would signify nothing at all. Nor did he now hope for a better opportunity, or more ability hereafter, as he had formerly done, because he saw and was fully convinced his own strength would for ever fail.

While he was musing in this manner, he saw, he said, with his heart (which is a common phrase among them) something that was unspeakably good and lovely, and what he had never seen before; and "this stole away his heart whether he would or no." He did not know what it was he saw. He did not say, "This is Jesus Christ"; but it was such glory and beauty as he never saw before. He did not now give away his heart so as he had formerly intended and attempted to do, but it *went away of itself* after that glory he then discovered. He used to try to make a bargain with Christ, to give up his heart to Him, that he might have eternal life for it. But now he thought nothing about himself, or what would become of him hereafter; his mind was wholly taken up with the unspeakable excellency of what he then beheld. After some time he was wonderfully pleased with the way of salvation by Christ; so that it seemed unspeakably better to be saved altogether by the mere free grace of God in Christ, than to have any hand in saving himself. The consequence of this exercise is, that he appears to retain a sense and relish of divine things, and to maintain a life of seriousness and true religion.

*January* 28.—The Indians in these parts having in times past run themselves in debt by their excessive drinking, and some having taken the advantage and put them to trouble and charge by arresting sundry of them; it was supposed a great part of their hunting lands was much endangered, and might speedily be taken from them. Sensible that they could not subsist together in these parts, in order to their being a Christian congregation, if these lands should drop out of their hands, which was thought very likely, I thought it my duty to use my utmost endeavours to prevent so unhappy an event. And having acquainted the gentlemen concerned with this mission of this affair, according to the best information I could get of it, they thought it proper to expend the money they had been and still were collecting for the religious interests of the Indians (at least a part of it), for discharging their debts, and securing these lands, that there might be no entanglement lying upon them to hinder the settlement and hopeful enlargement of a Christian congregation of Indians in these parts. And having received orders from them, I answered in behalf of the Indians for eighty - two pounds five shillings, New Jersey currency, at eight shillings per ounce; and so prevented the difficulty in this respect.

As God has wrought a wonderful work of grace among these Indians, and now inclines others from remote places to fall in among them almost continually; and as He has opened a door for the prevention of the difficulty now mentioned, which seemed greatly to threaten their religious interests as well as worldly comfort; it may be hoped the Lord designs to establish a Church for Himself among them, and to hand down true religion to their posterity.

*January 30.*—Preached to the Indians from John iii. 16, 17. There was a solemn attention and some affection visible in the audience; several persons who had long been concerned for their souls seemed afresh excited and engaged in seeking after an interest in Christ. One with much concern afterwards told me, "his heart was so pierced with my preaching, he knew not where to turn or what to do."

*January* 31.—This day the person I had made choice of and engaged for a schoolmaster arrived among us, and was heartily welcomed by my people universally. I immediately distributed several dozen of primers among the children and young people.

*February* 1, 1745-6.—My schoolmaster entered upon his business among the Indians. He has generally about thirty children and young persons in his school in the daytime, and about fifteen married people in the evening. The number of the latter sort of persons being less than it would be, if they could be more constantly at home, and spare time from their necessary employments for an attendance upon these instructions.

In the evening catechised in my usual method. Towards the close of my discourse, a surprising power seemed to attend the Word, especially to some persons. One man considerably in years, who had been a remarkable drunkard, a conjurer and murderer, that was awakened some months before, was now brought to great extremity under his spiritual distress, so that he trembled for hours together, and apprehended himself just dropping into hell, without any power to rescue or relieve himself. Several others appeared under great concern as well as he, and solicitous to obtain a saving change.

*Lord's day, February 2.*—Preached from John v. 24, 25. There appeared some concern and affection in the assembly as usual. Towards night proceeded in my usual method of catechising. Observed my people more ready in answering the questions proposed to them than ever before. It is apparent they advance daily in doctrinal knowledge. But, what is still more desirable, the Spirit of God is yet operating among them, whereby experimental as well as speculative knowledge is propagated in their minds.

*February 5.* — Discoursed to a considerable number of the Indians in the evening; several of them appeared much affected and melted with divine things.

*February 8.*—Spent a considerable part of the day in visiting my people from house to house, and conversing with them about their souls' concern. Divers persons wept while I discoursed to them, and appeared concerned for nothing so much as for an interest in the great Redeemer. In the evening catechised as usual. Divine truth made some impression upon the audience, and was attended with an affectionate engagement of soul in some.

*Lord's day, February 9.* — Discoursed to my people from the story of the blind man, Mark x. 46–52. The Word of God seemed weighty and powerful upon the assembly at this time, and made considerable impressions upon many. Some in particular, who have generally been remarkably stupid and careless under the means of grace, were now awakened and wept affectionately. The most earnest attention, as well as tenderness and affection, appeared in the audience universally.

Baptized three persons, two adults and one child. The adults, I have reason to hope, were both truly pious. There was a considerable melting in the assembly, while I was discoursing particularly to the persons, and administering the ordinance. God has been pleased to own and bless the administration of this as well as of His other ordinances, among the Indians. Some have been powerfully awakened at seeing others baptized; others have obtained relief and comfort, just in the season when this ordinance has been administered.

Toward night catechised. God made this a powerful season to some, who were much affected, and former convictions were revived. There was likewise one, who had been a vile drunkard, remarkably awakened. He appeared to be in great anguish of soul, wept and trembled, and continued so to do till near midnight. There was also a poor heavy-laden soul, who had been long under spiritual distress, as constant and pressing as ever I saw, that was now brought to a comfortable calm, and seemed to be bowed and reconciled to divine sovereignty. She told me that "she now saw and felt it was right that God should do with her as He pleased; and her heart felt satisfied it should be so." Although of late she had often found her heart rise and quarrel with God because He would, if He pleased, send her to hell after all she had done or could do to save herself. She added that the heavy burden she had lain under was now removed; that she had tried to recover her concern and distress again (fearing that the Spirit of God was departing from her and would leave her wholly careless), but that she could not recover it; that she felt she never could do anything to save herself, but must perish for ever if Christ did not do all for her; that she did not deserve His help, and that it would be right if He should leave her to perish. But Christ could save her, though she could do nothing to save herself; and here she seemed to rest.

FORKS OF DELAWARE, IN PENNSYLVANIA, 1745–6.

*Lord's day, February* 16.—Knowing that many of the Indians in these parts were obstinately set against Christianity, and that some of them had refused to hear me preach in times past, I thought it might be proper to have a number of my religious people from Crossweeksung with me, in order to converse with them about religious matters; hoping it might be a means to convince them of the truth and importance of Christianity, to see and hear some of their own nation discoursing of divine things, and manifesting earnest desires that others might be brought out of heathenish darkness, as they themselves were.

Having taken half a dozen of the most serious and knowing persons for this purpose, I this day met with them and the Indians of this place (some of whom probably could not have been prevailed upon to attend the meeting, had it not been for these religious Indians that accompanied me), and preached to them. Some of them who had in times past been extremely averse to Christianity now behaved soberly, but others laughed and mocked. However, the Word of God fell with such weight and power that several seemed to be stunned, and expressed a willingness to *hear me again of these matters.*

Afterwards prayed with and addressed the white people present, and could not but observe some visible effects of the Word among them. After public worship, spent some time and took pains to convince those that mocked of the truth and importance of what I had been insisting upon; and so endeavoured to awaken their attention to divine truths. I had reason to think, from what I observed then and afterwards, that my endeavours took considerable effect upon one of the worst of them. Those few Indians then present, who used to be my hearers in these parts (some having removed from hence to Crossweeksung), seemed kindly disposed and glad to see me again, though they had been so much attacked by some of the opposing pagans that they were almost ashamed or afraid to manifest their friendship.

*February* 17.—Having spent much time in discoursing to the Indians in their respective houses, I got them together, and repeated and inculcated what I had before taught them. Afterwards discoursed to them from Acts viii. 5–8. A divine influence seemed to attend the Word. Some of the Indians here appeared to be somewhat awakened, and manifested a concern of mind by their earnest attention, tears and sobs. My people from Crossweeksung continued with them day and night, repeating and inculcating the truths I had taught them. They sometimes prayed and sang psalms among them; discoursing with each other in their hearing of the great things God had done for them and for the Indians from whence they came; which seemed (as my people told me) to take more effect upon them than when they directed their discourses immediately to them.

*February* 18.—Preached to an assembly of Irish people near fifteen miles distant from the Indians.

*February* 19.—Preached to the Indians again, after having spent considerable time in conversing with them more privately. There appeared a great solemnity, and some concern and affection among the Indians belonging to these parts, as well as a sweet melting among those who came with me. Several of the Indians here seemed to have their prejudices and aversion to Christianity removed, and appeared well-disposed and inclined to hear the Word of God.

*February* 20.—Preached to a small assembly of High Dutch people, who had seldom heard the Gospel, and some of them at least were very ignorant; but who have lately been put upon an enquiry after the way of salvation. They gave wonderful attention; some of them were much affected under the Word, and afterwards said that they never had been so much enlightened about the way of salvation in their whole lives before. They requested me to tarry with them, or come again and preach to them. It grieved me that I could not comply with their request, for I could not but be affected with their circumstances; they being as *sheep not having a shepherd,* and some of them appearing under trouble of soul, standing in peculiar need of the assistance of an experienced spiritual guide.

*February* 21.—Preached to a number of people, many of them Low Dutch. Several of the forementioned High Dutch attended the sermon, though eight or ten miles distant from their houses. The Indians also belonging to these parts came of their own accord with my people from Crossweeksung to the meeting. Two in particular, who the last Sabbath opposed and ridiculed Christianity, were now present and behaved soberly. May the present encouraging appearance continue!

*February* 22.—Preached to the Indians. They appeared more free from prejudice, more cordial to

Christianity than before, and some of them much affected.

*Lord's day, February 23.* — Preached to the Indians from John vi. 35–37. After public service, discoursed particularly with several, and invited them to go down to Crossweeksung and tarry there at least for some time ; knowing they would then be free from the scoffs and temptations of the opposing pagans, as well as in the way of hearing divine truths discoursed of, both in public and private. I got a promise from some of them that they would speedily pay us a visit, and attend upon further instruction. They seem to be considerably enlightened, and freed from their prejudices against Christianity. But it is much to be feared their prejudices will revive again, unless they could enjoy the means of instruction here, or be removed where they might be under such advantages, and out of the way of their pagan acquaintance.

CROSSWEEKSUNG, IN NEW JERSEY, 1745-6.

*March 1.*—Catechised in my ordinary method. Was pleased and refreshed to see them answer the questions with such remarkable readiness, discretion, and knowledge. Towards the close of my discourse, divine truth made considerable impressions upon the audience. It produced tears and sobs in some under concern, and more especially a sweet and humble melting in others, whom I have reason to hope were truly gracious.

*Lord's day, March 2.*—Preached from John xv. 1–6. The assembly appeared not so lively in their attention as usual, nor so much affected with divine truth as has been common. Some of my people who went up to the Forks of Delaware with me, being now returned, were accompanied by two of the Indians belonging to the Forks, who had promised me a speedy visit. May the Lord meet with them here! They can scarcely go into a house now, but they will meet with Christian conversation ; and it is hopeful they may be both instructed and awakened.

Discoursed to the Indians again in the afternoon, and observed among them some liveliness and engagement in divine service, though not equal to what has often appeared here. I know of no assembly of Christians where there seems to be so much of the presence of God, where brotherly love so much prevails, and where I should take so much delight in public worship in the general, as in my own congregation ; although not more than nine months ago, they were worshipping devils and dumb idols under the power of pagan darkness and superstition. Amazing change this! effected by nothing less than divine power and grace. *This is the Lord's doing, and it is marvellous in our eyes!*

*March 5.*—Spent some time just at evening in prayer, singing, and discoursing to my people upon divine things ; and observed some agreeable tenderness and affection among them. Their present.

situation is so compact and commodious, that they are easily and quickly called together with only the sound of a conch-shell (a shell like that of a periwinkle), so that they have frequent opportunities of attending religious exercises publicly; which seems to be a great means, under God, of keeping alive the impressions of divine things in their mind.

*March* 8. — Catechised in the evening. My people answered the questions proposed to them well. I can perceive their knowledge in religion increases daily. And, what is still more desirable, the divine influence that has been so remarkable among them appears still to continue in some good measure. The divine presence seemed to be in the assembly this evening. Some, who I have good reason to think are Christians indeed, were melted with a sense of the divine goodness and their own barrenness and ingratitude, and seemed to hate themselves, as one of them afterwards expressed it. Convictions also appeared to be revived in several instances; and divine truths were attended with such influence upon the assembly in general, that it might justly be called an evening of divine power.

*Lord's day, March* 9.—Preached from Luke x. 38–42. The Word of God was attended with power and energy, and numbers were concerned to obtain the one thing needful. Some, who gave good evidences of their being truly gracious, were much affected with a sense of their want of spirituality, and saw the need they stood in of growing in grace; and most that had been under any impressions of divine things in time past, seemed now to have those impressions revived. In the afternoon proposed to have catechised in my usual method; but, while we were engaged in the first prayer in the Indian language, a great part of the assembly was so much moved and affected with divine things, that I thought it reasonable and proper to omit the proposing of questions for that time, and insist upon the most practical truths. I accordingly did so; making a further improvement of that passage of Scripture I discoursed upon in the former part of the day. There appeared to be a powerful divine influence in the congregation. Some that I have reason to think are truly pious were so deeply affected with a sense of their own barrenness, and their unworthy treatment of the blessed Redeemer, that they looked on Him as pierced by themselves and mourned, yea, some of them were *in bitterness as for a first-born*. Some poor awakened sinners also appeared to be in anguish of soul to obtain an interest in Christ. So that there was a great mourning in the assembly; many heavy groans, sobs, and tears; and one or two persons newly come among us were considerably awakened.

Methinks it would have refreshed the heart of any who truly love Zion's interest to have witnessed these glorious effects both upon saints and sinners. The place of worship appeared both solemn and sweet; and was so endeared by a display of the divine presence and grace, that those who had any relish of divine things could not but cry, *How amiable are Thy tabernacles, O Lord of hosts!*

After public worship was over, numbers came to my house, where we sang and discoursed; and the presence of God seemed here also to be in the midst of us. While we were singing, there was one (the woman mentioned in my Journal of February 9), who, I may venture to say, if I may be allowed to say so much of any person I ever saw, was *filled with joy unspeakable and full of glory*, and could not but burst forth in prayer and praises to God before us all, with many tears, crying, "O blessed Lord, do come, do come; O, do take me away, do let me die and go to Jesus Christ!—I am afraid if I live, I shall sin again! O, do let me die now! O dear Jesus, do come! I cannot stay, I cannot stay! O, how can I live in this world? do take my soul away from this sinful place! O, let me never sin any more! O, what shall I do, what shall I do? dear Jesus, O dear Jesus!" In this ecstasy she continued some time, uttering these and such like expressions incessantly; and the grand argument she used with God to take her away immediately was that, "if she lived, she should sin against Him."

When she had a little recovered herself, I asked her whether Christ was not now sweet to her soul. Turning to me with tears in her eyes, and with all the tokens of deep humility I ever saw in any person, she said, "I have many times heard you speak of the goodness and preciousness of Christ, that He was better than all the world; but O, I knew nothing what you meant, I never believed you! But now I know it is true:"—or words to that effect. I answered, And do you see enough in Christ for the greatest of sinners? She replied, "O, enough, enough, for all the sinners in the world if they would but come." And when I asked her, if she could not tell them of the goodness of Christ; turning herself round to some poor Christless souls who stood by, and were much affected, she said, "O, there is enough in Christ for you, if you would but come! O, strive, strive to give up your hearts to Him!" On hearing something of the glory of heaven mentioned, that there was no sin in that world, she again fell into the same ecstasy of joy, and desire of Christ's coming; repeating her former expressions, "O dear Lord, do let me go! O, what shall I do, what shall I do? I want to go to Christ; I cannot live; O, do let me die!"

She continued in this sweet frame for more than two hours, before she was able to get home. There may indeed be great joys arising even to an ecstasy, where there is still no substantial evidence of their being well - grounded. But in the present case there seemed to be no evidence wanting, in order to prove this joy to be divine, either in regard of its preparatives, attendants, or consequents. Of all the persons I have seen under spiritual exercise, I scarce ever saw one more bowed and broken under convictions of sin and misery than this woman; nor any who seem to have a greater acquaintance with her own heart. She would frequently complain to me of the hardness and rebellion of her heart; would tell me that her heart rose and quarrelled with God, when she thought He would do with her as He pleased, and send her to hell notwithstanding her prayers and good frames. That her heart was not willing to come to Christ for salvation, but tried everywhere else for help.

As she had been remarkably sensible of her stubbornness and contrariety to God under conviction, so she appeared to be no less remarkably bowed and reconciled to divine sovereignty before she obtained any relief or comfort. Something of this I have before noticed in my Journal of February 9. Since which time she has seemed constantly to breathe the spirit and temper of the new creature; crying after Christ, not through fear of hell as before, but with strong desires after Him as her only satisfying portion; and has many times wept and sobbed bitterly, because (as she apprehended) she did not and could not love Him. When I have sometimes asked her, Why she appeared so sorrowful, and whether it was because she was afraid of hell? she would answer, "No, I be not distressed about that; but my heart is so wicked I cannot love Christ"; and then she would burst out into tears. But though this has been the habitual frame of her mind for several weeks together, so that the exercise of grace appeared evident to others, yet she seemed wholly insensible of it herself, and never had any remarkable comfort or sensible satisfaction till this evening.

This sweet and surprising ecstasy appeared to spring from a true spiritual discovery of the glory, ravishing beauty and excellency of Christ, and not from any gross imaginary notions of His human nature; such as that of seeing Him in such a place or posture, as hanging on the Cross, as bleeding, dying, as gently smiling, and the like; which delusions some have been carried away with. Nor did it rise from a sordid selfish apprehension of her having any benefit whatsoever conferred on her, but from a view of His personal excellency and transcendent loveliness, which drew forth those vehement desires after Him, and made her long to be *absent from the body that she might be present with the Lord.*

The attendants of this ravishing comfort were such as abundantly discovered its spring to be divine, and that it was truly a *joy in the Holy Ghost.* Now she viewed divine truths as living realities; and could say, "I know these things are so, I feel they are true." Now her soul was resigned to the divine will in the most tender points; so that, when I said to her, What if God should take away your husband from you (who was then very sick), how do you think you could bear that? she replied, "He belongs to God and not to me; He may do with him just what He pleases." Now she had the most tender sense of the evil of sin, and discovered the utmost aversion to it; longing to die that she might be delivered from it. Now she could freely trust her all with God for time and eternity. And when I queried with her, how she could be willing to die, and leave her little infant; and what she thought would become of it in case she should? she answered, "God will take care of it. It belongs to Him, He will take care of it." Now she appeared to have the most humbling sense of her own meanness and unworthiness, her weakness and inability to preserve herself from sin and to persevere in the way of holiness, crying, "If I live, I shall sin." I thought I had never seen such an appearance of ecstasy and humility meeting in any one person in all my life before. The consequents of this joy are no less desirable and satisfactory than its attendants. She since appears to be a most tender, broken-hearted, affectionate, devout and humble Christian, as exemplary in life and conversation as any person in my congregation. May she still *grow in grace and in the knowledge of Christ!*

*March* 10. — Toward night the Indians met

together of their own accord, and sang, prayed, and discoursed of divine things among themselves. There was much affection among them; some who are hopefully gracious appeared to be melted with divine things; and others seemed much concerned for their souls. Perceiving their engagement and affection in religious exercises, I went among them and prayed, and gave a word of exhortation. I observed two or three somewhat affected and concerned, who scarcely ever appeared to be under any religious impressions before. It seemed to be a time of divine power. Numbers retained the warm impressions of divine things that had been made upon their minds the day before.

*March* 14.—Was visited by a considerable number of my people, and spent some time in religious exercises with them.

*March* 15. — In the evening catechised; they answered the questions put to them with surprising readiness and judgment. There appeared some warmth and feeling sense of divine things among those whom I have reason to hope are real Christians, while I was discoursing upon peace of conscience and joy in the Holy Ghost. These seemed quickened and enlivened, though there was not so much apparent concern among those whom I have reason to think in a Christless state.

*Lord's day, March* 16.—Preached to my congregation from Hebrews ii. 1–3. Divine truth seemed to have considerable influence upon many of the hearers, and produced many tears, as well as heavy sighs and sobs, among both those who have given evidence of being real Christians and others also. And the impressions made upon the audience appeared in general deep and heart-affecting, not noisy or superficial. Towards night discoursed on the *great salvation*. The Word was again attended with some power upon the audience. Numbers wept affectionately and to appearance unfeignedly; so that the Spirit of God seemed to be moving upon the face of the assembly.

Baptized the woman particularly mentioned in my Journal of last Lord's day; who now, as well as then, appeared to be in a devout, humble, and excellent frame of mind. My house being thronged with people in the evening, I spent the time in religious exercises with them, till my nature was almost spent. They are so unwearied in religious exercises, and insatiable in their thirsting after Christian knowledge, that I can sometimes scarcely avoid labouring so as greatly to exhaust my strength and spirits.

*March* 19.—Several persons who went with me to the Forks of Delaware in February last, having been detained there by the dangerous illness of one of their company, did not return home till this day. My people immediately met together of their own accord, in order to spend some time in religious exercises; especially to give thanks to God for His preserving goodness to those who have been absent from them for several weeks, and recovering mercy to him that had been sick; and that He had now returned them all in safety. I being then absent, they desired my schoolmaster to assist them in carrying on their religious solemnity; who tells me they appeared engaged and affectionate in repeated prayer and singing.

*March* 22.—Catechised in my usual method in the evening; the people answered questions to my great satisfaction. There appeared nothing very remarkable in the assembly, considering what has been common among us. Yet I may justly say the strict attention, the tenderness and affection, the many tears and heart-affecting sobs appearing in numbers in the assembly would have been very remarkable, were it not that God has made these things common with us, and even with strangers, soon after their coming amongst us. So far from thinking that every appearance and particular instance of affection amongst us has been truly genuine, and purely from a divine influence, I am sensible of the contrary; and doubt not but there have been some corrupt mixtures, some chaff as well as wheat, especially since religious concern became so common and prevalent here.

*Lord's day, March* 23.—About fifteen strangers having come amongst us in the week past, several of whom had never been in any religious meeting till now, I thought it proper to discourse this day in a manner peculiarly suited to their circumstances and capacities; and accordingly attempted it from Hosea xiii. 9. In the forenoon, I opened in the plainest manner I could, man's apostasy and ruined state, after having spoken some things respecting the being and perfections of God, and His creation of man in a state of innocence and happiness. In the afternoon, endeavoured to open the glorious provision God has made for the redemption of apostate creatures, by giving His own dear Son to suffer for them, and satisfy divine justice on their behalf.

There was not that affection and concern in the assembly which has been common among us, although there was a desirable attention appearing in general, and even in most of the strangers. Near sunset I felt an uncommon concern upon my mind, especially for the poor strangers, that God had so much withheld His presence and the powerful influence of His Spirit from the assembly in the exercises of the day. In this frame I visited their houses, and discoursed with some concern and affection to several persons particularly; but without much appearance of success, till I came to a house where some of the strangers were. There the solemn truths I discoursed of appeared to take effect, first upon some children, then upon adult persons that had been somewhat awakened before, and afterwards upon several of the pagan strangers.

I continued my discourse with some fervency, till almost every one in the house was melted into tears. Several wept aloud, and appeared earnestly concerned to obtain an interest in Christ. Numbers soon gathered from all the houses round about, and so thronged the place that we were obliged to remove to the house where we usually meet for public worship. The congregation gathering immediately, and many appearing remarkably affected, I discoursed some time from Luke xix. 10 ; endeavouring to open the mercy, compassion, and concern of Christ for lost, helpless, and undone sinners. There was much visible concern and affection in the assembly ; and I doubt not but that a divine influence accompanied what was spoken to the hearts of many. Five or six of the strangers, men and women, appeared to be considerably awakened ; and in particular one very rugged young man, who seemed as if nothing would move him, was now brought to tremble like the jailer and weep for a long time.

The awakened strangers seemed at once to put off their savage roughness and pagan manners, and became sociable, orderly, and humane in their carriage. When they first came, I exhorted my religious people to take pains with them (as they had done with other strangers from time to time) to instruct them in Christianity. But when they attempted something of that nature, the strangers would soon rise up and walk to other houses, in order to avoid the hearing of such discourse. Several of the serious persons accordingly agreed to disperse themselves into the several parts of the settlement; so that, wherever the strangers went, they met with some instructive discourse, and warm addresses respecting their souls' concern. But now there was no need of using policy in order to get an opportunity of conversing with them; for they were so far touched with a sense of their perishing state as made them yield to the closest addresses respecting their sin and misery, their need of an acquaintance with and interest in the great Redeemer.

*March* 24. — Numbered the Indians, to see how many souls God had gathered together here, since my coming into these parts; and found there was now about a hundred and thirty, old and young. About fifteen or twenty of my stated hearers were absent at this season; so that if all had been together, the number would now have been very considerable; especially considering how few were together at my first coming into these parts, the whole number not amounting to ten persons.

My people are going out this day upon the design of clearing some of their lands above fifteen miles distant from this settlement, in order to their settling there in a compact form, where they might enjoy the advantages of attending the public worship of God, of having their children schooled, and at the same time have a conveniency for planting; their land in the place of our present residence being of little or no value for that purpose. The design of their settling thus in a body, and cultivating their lands (which they have done very little at in their pagan state) being of such necessity and importance to their religious interest, as well as worldly comfort, I thought it proper to call them together, and show them the duty of labouring with faithfulness and industry; and that they must not now be *slothful in business,* as they had ever been in their pagan state. I endeavoured to press the importance of their being laborious, diligent, and vigorous in the prosecution of their business, especially at the present juncture (the season of planting being now near), in order to their being in a capacity of living together, and enjoying the means of grace and instruction. And having given them directions for their work, which they very much wanted, as well as for their behaviour in divers respects, I explained, .sang, and endeavoured to inculcate upon them Psalm cxxvii., common metre, Dr. Watts's version. I then commended them and the design of their going forth to God by prayer, and dismissed them to their business.

In the evening read and expounded to those of them who were yet at home, and the strangers newly come, the substance of the third chapter of the Acts. Numbers seemed to melt under the Word, especially while I was discoursing upon verse 19. The strangers also were affected. When I asked them afterwards whether they did not now feel that their hearts were wicked, as I had taught them; one replied, " Yes, she felt it now." Although before she came here (upon hearing that I taught the Indians their hearts were all bad by nature, and needed to be changed and made good by the power of God), she had said, " Her heart was not wicked, and she never had done anything that was bad in her life." This indeed seems to be the case with them universally in their pagan state. They have no consciousness of sin and guilt, unless they can charge themselves with some gross acts of sin contrary to the commands of the second table.

*March* 27.—Discoursed to a number of my people in one of their houses in a more private manner. Enquired particularly into their spiritual state, in order to see what impressions of a religious nature they were under. Laid before them the marks and tokens of a regenerate as well as an unregenerate state; and endeavoured to suit my discourse to them severally, according as I apprehended their states to be. A considerable number gathered together before I finished my discourse, and several seemed much affected, while I was urging the necessity and infinite importance of a renewed state. I find particular and close dealing with souls in private is often very successful.

*March* 29.—In the evening catechised as usual. Treated upon the "benefits which believers receive from Christ at death." The questions were answered with great readiness and propriety; and those who, I hope, are the people of God were in general sweetly melted. There appeared such a liveliness and vigour in their attendance upon the Word, and such eagerness to be made partakers of the benefits then mentioned, that they seemed to be not only *looking for, but hastening to the coming of the day of God.* Divine truth seemed to distil upon the audience with a gentle but melting efficacy, as the refreshing *showers upon the new mown grass.* The assembly in general, as well as those who appear truly religious, were affected with some brief account of the blessedness of the godly at death; and discovered an affectionate inclination to cry, *Let me die the death of the righteous.* Yet many were not duly engaged to obtain the change of heart that is necessary in order to that blessed end.

*Lord's day, March* 30.—Discoursed from Matthew xxv. 31–40. There was a very considerable moving and affectionate melting in the assembly, and I hope there were some real, deep, and abiding impressions of divine things made upon the minds of many. One aged man, newly come amongst us, appeared to be considerably awakened, but who never was touched with any concern for his soul before. In the evening catechised.

There was not that tenderness and melting among God's people that appeared the evening before, and at many other times. Yet they answered the questions distinctly and well, and were devout and attentive in divine service.

*March* 31.—Called my people together, as I had done the Monday morning before, and discoursed to them again on the necessity and importance of their labouring industriously, in order to their living together and enjoying the means of grace; and having engaged in solemn prayer to God among them for a blessing upon their attempts, I dismissed them to their work. Numbers of them, both men and women, seemed to offer themselves willingly to this service; and some appeared affectionately concerned that God might go with them and begin their little town for them; that by His blessing it might be comfortable for them and theirs, in regard both of procuring the necessaries of life and attending the worship of God.

*April* 5, 1746.—Catechised towards evening. There appeared to be some affection and fervency in the assembly in general, especially towards the conclusion of my discourse. After public worship, a number of the truly religious came to my house, and seemed eager for some further entertainment upon divine things. While I was conversing with them about their spiritual exercises, observing to them that God's work in the hearts of all His children was for substance the same, and that their

trials and temptations were also alike, and showing the obligations such were under to love one
another in a peculiar manner, they seemed to be
melted into tenderness and affection toward each
other. I thought that particular token of their
being the disciples of Christ, of their *having love
one toward another*, had scarcely ever appeared
more evident than at this time.

*Lord's day, April 6.*—Preached from Matthew
vii. 21–23. There were considerable effects of the
Word visible in the audience, and such as were
very desirable; an earnest attention, a great
solemnity, many tears and heavy sighs, which were
modestly suppressed in a considerable measure,
and appeared unaffected, without any indecent
commotion of the passions. Several religious
people were put upon serious and close examina-
tion, from hearing that *not every one that saith to
Christ, Lord, Lord, shall enter into His kingdom.*
Some of them expressed fears lest they had
deceived themselves with a false hope, because
they found they had done so little of the *will of
His Father who is in heaven.* One man was brought
under very great and pressing concern for his soul,
which appeared more especially after his retirement from public worship. That which gave him
his great uneasiness, he says, was not so much any
particular sin, as that he had never done the will
of God at all but had sinned continually, and so
had no claim to the kingdom of heaven. In the

afternoon I opened to them the discipline of Christ in His Church, and the method in which offenders are to be dealt with. The religious people were much affected when they heard that the offender continuing obstinate must finally be esteemed and treated *as a heathen man,* a pagan, that has no part nor lot among God's visible people. *This* they seemed to have the most awful apprehensions of; a state of heathenism, out of which they were so lately brought, appearing very dreadful to them. After public worship I visited several houses to see how they spent the remainder of the Sabbath, and to treat with them solemnly on the great concerns of their souls. The Lord seemed to smile upon my private endeavours, and to make these personal addresses more effectual upon some than my public discourses.

*April 7.*—Preached to my people in the evening from 1 Corinthians xi. 23–26. Endeavoured to open to them the institution, nature, and ends of the Lord's Supper, as well as the qualifications and preparations necessary to the right participation of that ordinance. Several appeared much affected with the love of Christ, in making this provision for the comfort of His people, at a season when Himself was just entering upon His sharpest sufferings.

*Lord's day, April 20.*—Discoursed both forenoon and afternoon from Luke xxiv., explaining most of the chapter, and making remarks upon it. There was a desirable attention in the audience, though not so much appearance of affection and tenderness among them as has been usual. Our meeting was very full; some strangers were present who had never been with us before.

In the evening catechised. My people answered the questions proposed to them readily and distinctly; and I could perceive they advanced in their knowledge of the principles of Christianity. There was an affectionate melting in the assembly at this time. Several of the truly religious were refreshed and quickened, and seemed by their discourse and behaviour after public worship to have their *hearts knit together in love.* This was a blessed season, like many others that my poor people have been favoured with in months past. God has caused *this little fleece* to be repeatedly wet with the blessed *dews* of divine grace, while all the earth around has been comparatively dry.

*April 25.*—Having of late apprehended that a number of persons in my congregation were proper subjects of the ordinance of the Lord's Supper, and that it might be seasonable speedily to administer it to them; and having taken advice of some of the Correspondents in this solemn affair, and accordingly proposed and appointed the next Lord's day (with leave of divine Providence) for the administration of this ordinance, this day was set apart for solemn fasting and prayer, to implore the blessing of God upon our design of renewing covenant with Him and with one another, to walk together in the fear of God, in love and Christian fellowship; and to entreat that His divine presence might be with us in our designed approach to His table, as well as to humble ourselves before God on account of the apparent withdrawment (at least in a measure) of that blessed influence which has been so prevalent upon persons of all ages among us; as also on account of the rising appearance of carelessness, vanity, and vice among some, who some time since appeared to be touched and affected with divine truths, and brought to some sensibility of their miserable and perishing state by nature. And that we might also importunately pray for the peaceable settlement of the Indians together in a body, that they might be a commodious congregation for the worship of God; and that God would defeat all the attempts that were or might be made against that pious design.[1]

The solemnity was observed and seriously attended, not only by those who proposed to communicate at the Lord's Table, but by the whole congregation. In the former part of the day, I

[1] There being at this time a terrible clamour raised against the Indians in various places in the country, and insinuations as though I was training them up to cut people's throats. Numbers wishing to have them banished out of these parts, and some giving out great swelling words, in order to fright and deter from settling upon the best and most convenient tract of their own lands, threatening to molest and trouble them in the law, pretending a claim to these lands themselves, although never purchased of the Indians.

endeavoured to open to my people the nature and
design of a fast, as I had attempted more briefly to
do before, and to instruct them in the duties of
such a solemnity.   In the afternoon I insisted upon
the special reasons there were for our engaging in
these solemn exercises at this time, both in regard
to our need of divine assistance in order to a due
preparation for that sacred ordinance we were some
of us proposing speedily to attend upon, and also
in respect to the manifest decline of God's work
here as to the effectual conviction and conversion
of sinners, there having been few of late deeply
awakened out of a state of security.

The worship of God was attended with great
solemnity and reverence, with much tenderness
and many tears, by those who appear to be truly
religious.   There was also some appearance of
divine power upon those who had been awakened
some time before, and who were still under concern.   After repeated prayer and attendance upon
the Word of God, I proposed to the religious
people, with as much brevity and plainness as I
could, the substance of the doctrine of the Christian
faith, as I had formerly done previous to their
baptism, and had their renewed cheerful assent to
it.   I then led them to a solemn renewal of their
baptismal covenant, wherein they had explicitly
and publicly given up themselves to God, the
Father, Son, and Holy Ghost, avouching Him to
be their God ; and at the same time renouncing

their idolatrous and superstitious practices, and solemnly engaging to take the Word of God, so far as it was or might be made known to them, for the rule of their lives, promising to walk together in love, to watch over themselves and one another; to lead lives of seriousness and devotion, and to discharge the relative duties incumbent upon them respectively.

This solemn transaction was attended with much gravity and seriousness, and at the same time with the utmost readiness, freedom, and cheerfulness. A religious union and harmony of soul seemed to crown the whole solemnity. I could not but think in the evening, that there had been manifest tokens of the divine presence with us in all the services of the day; though it was also manifest there was not that concern among Christless souls which has often appeared here.

*April* 26.—Toward noon prayed with a dying child and gave a word of exhortation to the by-standers to prepare for death, which seemed to take effect upon some. In the afternoon discoursed to my people from Matthew xxvi. 26–30, of the Author, the nature and design of the Lord's Supper; and endeavoured to point out the worthy receivers of that ordinance. The religious people were affected, and even melted with a view of the dying love of Christ. Others who had been for some months under convictions of their perishing state appeared now to be much moved with concern, and afresh engaged in seeking after an interest in Christ; though I cannot say that the Word of God appeared so *quick and powerful,* so sharp and piercing to the assembly, as it had sometimes formerly done.

Baptized two adult persons, both serious and exemplary in their lives, and I hope truly religious. One of them was the man particularly mentioned in my Journal of the 6th instant; who, though he was then greatly distressed, because "he had never done the will of God," has since, we hope, obtained spiritual comfort upon good grounds.

In the evening I catechised those that were designed to partake of the Lord's Supper the next day, explaining the institution, nature, and end of that ordinance; and had abundant satisfaction respecting their doctrinal knowledge and fitness in that respect for an attendance upon it. They likewise appeared in general to have an affecting view of the solemnity of this sacred ordinance, to be humbled under a sense of their own unworthiness to approach to God in it, and to be earnestly concerned that they might be duly prepared for an attendance upon it. Their hearts were full of love one toward another, and that was the frame of mind they seemed much concerned to maintain and bring to the Lord's Table with them. In singing and prayer, after catechising, there appeared an agreeable tenderness and melting among them, and such tokens of brotherly love and affection that would even constrain one to say, *Lord, it is good to be here*; it is good to dwell where such a heavenly influence distils.

*Lord's day, April 27.*—Preached from Titus ii. 14, *Who gave Himself for us*, etc. The Word of God was attended with some appearance of divine power upon the assembly; the attention and gravity of the audience was remarkable; and, towards the conclusion especially, several persons were much affected.

Administered the Lord's Supper to twenty-three of the Indians, the number of men and women being nearly equal. Five or six others were now absent at the Forks of Delaware, who would otherwise have communicated with us. The ordinance was attended with great solemnity, and with a most desirable tenderness and affection. It was remarkable that during the sacramental actions, especially in the distribution of the bread, they seemed to be affected in a most lively manner, as if Christ had been really *crucified before them*. And the words of the institution, when repeated and enlarged upon in the administration, seemed to meet with the same reception, to be entertained with the same full and firm belief and affectionate engagement of soul, as if the Lord Jesus Christ Himself had been present and had personally spoken to them. The affections of the communicants, though considerably raised, were notwithstanding agreeably regulated and kept within proper bounds. There was a sweet, gentle, and affectionate melting, without any boisterous commotion of the passions.

Having rested some time after the administration of the sacrament, I walked from house to house, and conversed particularly with most of the communicants, and found they had been almost universally refreshed at the Lord's Table *as with new wine.* Never did I see such an appearance of Christian love among any people in all my life. It was so remarkable that one might well have cried with an agreeable surprise, *Behold how they love one another.* I think there could be no greater tokens of mutual affection among the people of God in the early days of Christianity than what now appeared here. The sight was so desirable, and so well becoming the Gospel, that nothing less could be said of it than that it was *the doing of the Lord,* the genuine operations of Him who is Love itself.

Towards night discoursed again on the forementioned Titus ii. 14, and insisted on the immediate end and design of Christ's death, *that He might redeem His people from all iniquity.* This also appeared to be a season of divine power amongst us. The religious people were much refreshed, and seemed remarkably tender and affectionate, full of love, joy, peace, and desires of being completely *redeemed from all iniquity*; some of them afterwards told me, "they had never felt the like before." Convictions also appeared to be revived in many instances; and several were awakened, whom I had never observed under any religious impressions before.

Such was the influence that attended our assembly, and so unspeakably desirable the frame of mind that many enjoyed in the divine service, that it seemed almost grievous to conclude the public worship. The congregation when dismissed, though it was then almost dark, appeared loth to leave the place and employments that had been rendered so dear to them by the benefits enjoyed, while a blessed quickening influence distilled upon them. Upon the whole I must say, I had great satisfaction in the administration of this ordinance. I have abundant reason to think that those who came to the Lord's Table had a good degree of doctrinal knowledge of the nature and design of the ordinance, and that they acted understandingly in what they did.

In the preparatory services I found uncommon freedom in opening to their understandings and capacities the covenant of grace, and in showing them the nature of this ordinance as a seal of that covenant; though many of them knew of no such thing as a seal before my coming among them, or at least of the use and design of it in the common affairs of life. They were likewise thoroughly sensible that it was no more than a seal or sign, and not the real body and blood of Christ; that it was designed for the refreshment and edification of the soul and not for the feasting of the body. They were also acquainted with the end of the ordinance, that they were therein called to commemorate the dying love of Christ.

This competency of doctrinal knowledge, together with their grave and decent attendance upon the ordinance, their affectionate melting under it, and the sweet and Christian frame of mind they discovered afterwards, gave me great satisfaction. O what a blessed season was this! God Himself, I am persuaded, was in the midst of His people, attending His own ordinances. I doubt not but many in the conclusion of the day could say with their whole hearts, *Verily, a day thus spent in God's house is better than a thousand elsewhere.* There seemed to be but one heart among the pious people. The union, harmony, and endearing love and tenderness subsisting among them, were, I thought, the most lively emblem of the heavenly world I had ever seen.

*April* 28.—Concluded the sacramental solemnity with a discourse from John xiv. 15, *If ye love Me, keep My commandments.* There appeared a very agreeable tenderness in the audience in general, but especially in the communicants. How free, how engaged and affectionate did these appear in the service of God! They seemed willing to have their *ears bored to the door posts* of God's house, and to be His servants for ever.

Observing numbers in this excellent frame, and the assembly in general affected by a divine influence, I thought it proper to improve this advantageous season, as Hezekiah did the desirable season of his great passover, in order to promote the blessed reformation begun among them, and engage those that appear serious and religious to persevere therein. I accordingly proposed to them that they should renewedly enter into covenant before God, that they would watch over themselves and one another, lest they should dishonour the name of Christ by falling into sinful and un-becoming practices. Especially that they would watch against the sin of drunkenness, the sin that easily besets them, and the temptations lead-ing to it, as well as *the appearance of evil* in that respect. They cheerfully complied with the pro-posal, and explicitly joined in that covenant. I therefore proceeded in the most solemn manner I could, to call God to witness respecting their sacred engagement; reminding them of the great-ness of the guilt they would contract in the violation of it, and that God would be a terrible witness against those who should presume to do so, in the *great and notable day of the Lord.*

It was a season of amazing solemnity; a divine awe appeared upon the face of the whole assembly in this transaction. Affectionate sobs, sighs, and tears were now frequent in the audience; and I doubt not but that many silent cries were then sent up to the Fountain of grace, for supplies of grace sufficient for the fulfilment of these solemn engagements. Baptized six children this day.

*Lord's day, May 4.*—My people being now re-moved to their lands, mentioned in my Journal of March 24, where they have been making provision for a compact settlement, in order to their more convenient enjoyment of the Gospel and other means of instruction, as well as the comforts of life ; I this day visited them (being now obliged to board with an English family at some distance from them), and preached to them in the forenoon from Mark iv. 5. Endeavoured to show them the reason there was to fear lest many promising appearances and hopeful beginnings in religion might prove abortive, like the seed dropped upon stony places.

In the afternoon discoursed upon Romans viii. 9, *Now if any man have not the Spirit of Christ, he is none of His.* I have reason to think this discourse was peculiarly seasonable, and that it had a good effect upon some of the hearers. Spent some hours afterwards in private conferences with my people, and laboured to regulate some things I apprehended amiss among some of them.

*May 5.*—Visited them again, and took care of their worldly concerns, giving them directions relating to their business. I daily discover more and more of what importance it is to their religious interests that they become laborious and industrious, acquainted with the affairs of husbandry, and able in a good measure to raise the necessaries and comforts of life within themselves; for their present method of living greatly exposes them to temptations of various kinds.

*May 9.*—Preached from John v. 40, in the open wilderness; the Indians having as yet no house for public worship in this place, nor scarcely any shelter for themselves. Divine truth made considerable impressions upon the audience, and it was a season of solemnity, tenderness, and affection.

Baptized one man this day (the conjurer and murderer mentioned in my Journal of August 8, 1745, and February 1, 1745–6), who appears to be such a remarkable instance of divine grace, that I cannot omit some brief account of him here.

He lived near, and sometimes attended my meeting in the Forks of Delaware for more than a year together; but was, like many others of them, extremely attached to strong drink, and seemed to be no ways reformed by the means I used for their instruction and conversion. In this time he likewise murdered a likely young Indian, which threw him into some kind of horror and desperation, so that he kept at a distance from me, and refused to hear me preach for several months together, till I had an opportunity of conversing freely with him, and giving him encouragement that his sin might be forgiven for

Christ's sake. After which he sometimes attended the meeting.

But the worst part of all his conduct was his conjuration. He was one of them who are sometimes called Powwows among the Indians; and notwithstanding his frequent attendance upon my preaching, he still followed his old charms and juggling tricks, *giving out that himself was some great one, and to him they gave heed,* supposing him to be possessed of a *great power.* When I instructed them respecting the miracles wrought by Christ in healing the sick, and mentioned them as evidences of His divine mission and the truth of His doctrines, they quickly observed the wonders of that kind which this man had performed by his magic charms. Hence they had a high opinion of him and his superstitious notions, which seemed to be a fatal obstruction to some of them in regard of their receiving the Gospel. And I have often thought, it would be a great favour to the design of gospellising the Indians, if God would take that wretch out of the world; for I had scarcely any hope of his ever coming to good. But God, *whose thoughts are not as man's thoughts,* has been pleased to take a much more desirable method with him; a method agreeable to His own merciful nature, and, I trust, advantageous to His own interest among the Indians, as well as effectual to the salvation of the poor soul himself; and to Him be the glory of it.

The first genuine concern that ever appeared in him was excited by seeing my interpreter and his wife baptized at the Forks of Delaware, July 21, 1745. This so prevailed upon him that, with the invitation of an Indian who was a friend to Christianity, he followed me down to Crossweeksung in the beginning of August following, in order to hear me preach, and there continued for several weeks, in a season of the most remarkable and powerful awakening among the Indians. He was then more effectually awakened, and brought under great concern for his soul. Upon "feeling the Word of God in his heart," as he expresses it, his spirit of conjuration left him entirely; and he has had no more power of that nature since than any other man living. He declares that he does not now so much as know how he used to charm and conjure; and that he could not do anything of that nature, were he ever so desirous of it.

He continued under convictions of his sinful and perishing state all the fall and former part of the winter past, but was not so deeply exercised till some time in January; and then the Word of God took such hold upon him that he was brought into great distress, and knew not what to do nor where to turn himself. He then told me that, when he used to hear me preach from time to time in the fall of the year, my preaching pierced his heart and made him very uneasy, but did not bring him to so great distress, because he still hoped he could do something for his own relief.   But now, he said, I drove him up into "such a sharp corner" that he had no way to turn, and could not avoid being in distress.   He continued constantly under the heavy burden and pressure of a wounded spirit, till at length he was brought to the utmost agony of soul, mentioned in my Journal of February 1, which continued that night and part of the next day.

After this he enjoyed great calmness and composure of mind; his trembling and heavy burden were removed, and he appeared perfectly sedate; though he had, to his apprehension, scarcely any hope of salvation.   Observing him in this state, I asked him how he did.   He replied, " It is done, it is done, it is all done now."   I asked him what he meant.   He answered, " I can never do any more to save myself, it is all done for ever, I can do no more."   I queried with him, whether he could not do a little more rather than go to hell. He replied, " My heart is dead, I can never help myself."   I asked him what he thought would become of him then.   He answered, " I must go to hell."   I asked him whether he thought it was right God should send him there.   He replied, " O, it is right.   The devil has been in me ever since I was born."   I asked him whether he felt this, when he was in such great distress the evening before.   He answered, " No, I did not then think it was right.   I thought God would send me to hell, and that I was then dropping into it; but my heart quarrelled with God, and would not say it was right He should send me there. But now I know it is right, for I have always served the devil, and my heart has no goodness in it now, but is as bad as ever it was."

I thought I had scarcely ever seen any person more effectually brought off from a dependence upon his own contrivances and endeavours for salvation, or more apparently to lie at the foot of sovereign mercy, than this man now did under these views of things. In this frame of mind he continued for several days, passing sentence of condemnation upon himself, and constantly owning that it would be right he should be damned, and that he expected this would be his portion for the greatness of his sins. Yet it was plain he had a secret hope of mercy, though imperceptible to himself, which kept him not only from despair but from any pressing distress; so that, instead of being sad and dejected, his very countenance appeared pleasant and agreeable.

While in this frame, he asked me several times when I would preach again; and seemed desirous to hear the Word of God every day. I asked him why he wanted to hear me preach, seeing "his heart was dead, and all was done"; that "he could never help himself, and expected that he must go to hell." He replied, "I love to hear you speak about Christ for all." I added, But what good will that do you, if you must go to hell at last? I now

used his own language with him; having before
laboured in the best manner I could to represent
to him the excellency of Christ, His all-sufficiency
and willingness to save lost sinners and persons
just in his case, but without yielding him any
special comfort. He answered, "I would have
others come to Christ, if I must go to hell myself."
It was remarkable that at this time he seemed to
have a great love to the people of God, and nothing
affected him so much as the thoughts of being
separated from them. This seemed to be a very
dreadful part of hell he thought himself doomed
to. It was likewise remarkable that he was now
most diligent in the use of all means for his soul's
salvation, though he had the clearest view of the
insufficiency of means to afford him help. He
would frequently say, "That all he did signified
nothing at all"; yet he was never more constant
in doing, attending secret and family prayer daily,
and surprisingly diligent and attentive in hearing
the Word of God. Hence he neither despaired of
mercy, nor presumed to hope upon his own doings,
but used means, because appointed of God in order
to salvation, and because he would wait upon God
in His own way.

After continuing in this frame of mind more
than a week, while I was discoursing publicly, he
seemed to have a lively, soul-refreshing view of
the excellency of Christ and the way of salvation
by Him, which melted him into tears, and filled

him with admiration, comfort, satisfaction, and praise. He has since appeared to be a humble, devout, and affectionate Christian; serious and exemplary in his conversation and behaviour, frequently complaining of his barrenness, his want of spiritual warmth, life, and activity, and yet frequently favoured with quickening and refreshing influences. In all respects, so far as I am able to judge, he bears the marks and characters of one *created anew in Christ Jesus to good works.*

His zeal for the cause of God was pleasing, when he was with me at the Forks of Delaware in February last. An old Indian at the place where I preached threatened to bewitch me, and my religious people who accompanied me there. This man presently challenged him to do his worst, telling him that himself had been as great a conjurer as he, and that, notwithstanding, as soon as he felt that Word in his heart which these people loved (meaning the Word of God), his power of conjuring immediately left him. And so it would you, said he, if you did but once feel it in your heart; and you have no power to hurt them, nor so much as to touch one of them. I may conclude my account of him by observing, in allusion to what was said of St. Paul, that he now zealously defends and practically *preaches the faith which once he destroyed,* or at least was instrumental in obstructing. May God have the glory of the amazing change that is wrought in him!

*Lord's day, May* 18.—Discoursed both parts of the day from Revelation iii. 20. There appeared some affectionate melting towards the close of the forenoon exercise, and one or two instances of fresh awakening. In the intermission of public worship, I took occasion to discourse to numbers in a more private way on the kindness and patience of the blessed Redeemer in *standing and knocking,* in continuing His gracious calls to sinners, who had long neglected and abused His grace; which seemed to take effect upon some. In the afternoon divine truths were attended with solemnity and with some tears, though there was not that powerful awakening and quickening influence, which in times past has been common in our assemblies. The appearance of the audience was comparatively discouraging, and I was ready to fear that God was about to withdraw the blessed influence of His Spirit from us.

*May* 19.—Visited and preached to my people from Acts xx. 18, 19. Endeavoured to rectify their notions about religious affections; showing them, on the one hand, the desirableness of religious affection, tenderness, and fervent engagement in the worship and service of God, when such affection flows from a true spiritual discovery of divine glories, from a justly-affecting sense of the transcendent excellency and perfections of the blessed God,—a view of the glory and loveliness of the great Redeemer; and that such views of divine things will naturally excite us to *serve the Lord with many tears*, with much affection and fervency, and yet *with all humility of mind*. On the other hand, I observed the sinfulness of seeking after high affections immediately and for their own sakes, that is, of making them the object on which our heart is principally set, instead of the glory of God. I showed them that, if the heart be directly and chiefly fixed on God and engaged to glorify Him, some degree of religious affection will be the natural effect. But to seek after affection directly and chiefly, to have the heart principally set upon that, is to place it in the room of God and His glory. If it be sought, that others may take notice of and admire us for our spirituality and forwardness in religion, it is then abominable pride ; if for the sake of feeling the pleasure of being affected, it is then idolatry and self-gratification. I laboured also to expose the disagreeableness of those affections that are sometimes wrought up in persons by the power of fancy, and their own attempts for that purpose, while I still endeavoured to recommend to them that religious affection, fervency, and devotion which ought to attend all our religious exercises, and without which religion will be but an empty name and lifeless carcase.

This appeared to be a seasonable discourse, and proved very satisfactory to some of the religious people, who before were exercised with difficulties relating to this point.

*May* 24.—Visited the Indians, and took care of their secular business, which they are not able to manage themselves without the constant care and advice of others. Discoursed more particularly with some about their spiritual concerns.

*Lord's day, May* 25.—Preached both parts of the day from John xii. 44–48. Some degree of divine power attended the Word; several wept and appeared considerably affected; and one who had long been under spiritual trouble now obtained clearness and comfort, and appeared to rejoice in God her Saviour. It was a day of grace and goodness; a day wherein something I trust was done for the cause of God among the people. It was also a season of comfort to the godly, though there was not that powerful influence upon the congregation which was common some months ago.

*Lord's day, June* 1, 1746.—Preached both forenoon and afternoon from Matthew xi. 27, 28. The presence of God seemed to be in the assembly, and numbers were considerably melted and affected under the Word. There was a desirable appearance in the congregation in general, an earnest attention and agreeable tenderness, and it seemed as if God designed to visit us with further showers of divine grace. I then baptized ten persons, five adults and five children, and was not a little refreshed with this addition to the Church of such as I hope shall be saved. Since our celebration of the Lord's

Supper, several who had long been under spiritual trouble and concern have obtained relief and comfort, though there have been few instances of persons lately awakened out of a state of security. And those comforted of late seem to be brought in, in a more silent way, neither their concern nor consolation being so powerful and remarkable, as appeared among those more suddenly wrought upon in the beginning of this work of grace.

*June* 6.—Discoursed to my people from part of Isaiah liii. The divine presence appeared to be amongst us in some measure. Several persons were much melted and refreshed ; and one man in particular, who had long been under concern for his soul, was now brought to see and feel in a very lively manner the impossibility of his doing anything to help himself, or to bring him into the favour of God, by his tears, prayers, and other religious performances. He found himself undone as to any power or goodness of his own, and that there was no way left but to leave himself with God to be disposed of as He pleased.

*June* 7. — Being desired by the Rev. William Tennent to be his assistant in the administration of the Lord's Supper, my people also being invited to attend the sacramental solemnity, they cheerfully embraced the opportunity, and this day attended the preparatory services with me.

*Lord's day, June* 8.—Most of my people who had

been communicants at the Lord's Table before, being present at this sacramental occasion, communicated with others in this holy ordinance, at the desire and I trust to the satisfaction and comfort of numbers of God's people, who had longed to see this day, and whose hearts had rejoiced in this work of grace among the Indians, which prepared the way for what appeared so agreeable at this time. Those of my people who communicated seemed agreeably affected at the Lord's Table, and some of them considerably melted with the love of Christ; though they were not so remarkably refreshed and feasted at this time, as when I administered this ordinance to them in our own congregation only.

Some of the spectators were affected with seeing these, who had been *aliens from the commonwealth of Israel and strangers to the covenant of promise,* who of all men had lived *without God and without hope in the world,* now brought *near to God* as His professing people, and sealing covenant with Him by a solemn and devout attendance upon this sacred ordinance. And as numbers of God's people were refreshed with this sight, and thereby excited to bless God for the enlargement of His kingdom in the world, so some others (I was told) were awakened by it, apprehending the danger they were in of being themselves finally cast out, while they saw others, *from the east and west,* preparing, and hopefully prepared in some good measure, to *sit down in the kingdom of God.*

At this season, others of my people also, who were not communicants, were considerably affected ; convictions were revived in divers instances ; and one (the man particularly mentioned in my Journal of the 6th instant) obtained comfort and satisfaction ; and has since given me such an account of his spiritual exercises, and the manner in which he obtained relief, as appears very hopeful. It seems as if He *who commanded the light to shine out of darkness* had now *shined in his heart, and given him the light of* an experimental *knowledge of the glory of God in the face of Jesus Christ.*

*June 9.*—A considerable number of my people met together early in the day in a retired place in the woods, and prayed, sang, and conversed of divine things. They were seen by some religious persons of the white people to be affected and engaged, and several of them in tears in these religious exercises. They afterwards attended the concluding exercises of the sacramental solemnity, and then returned home, " rejoicing for all the goodness of God " they had seen and felt. This was a profitable and comfortable season to numbers of my congregation. A number of them communicating at the Lord's Table with others of God's people on this occasion, was I trust for the honour of God and the interest of religion in these parts, and many I hope were quickened by it.

*June* 13.—Preached to my people upon the new creature, from 2 Corinthians v. 17. The presence of God appeared to be in the assembly. It was a sweet and agreeable meeting; the people of God were refreshed and strengthened, beholding their faces in the glass of God's Word, and finding in themselves the marks and lineaments of the new creature. Some sinners under concern were also renewedly affected; and afresh engaged for the securing of their eternal interest.

Baptized five persons at this time, three adults and two children. One of them was the very aged woman, of whose exercise I gave an account in my Journal of December 26. She now gave me a very punctual, rational, and satisfactory account of the remarkable change she experienced some months after the beginning of her concern, which appeared to be the genuine operations of the divine Spirit, so far as I am capable of judging. And though she was become so childish through old age that I could do nothing in a way of questioning with her, nor scarce make her understand what I asked her; yet when I let her alone to go on with her own story, she could give a very distinct and particular relation of the various exercises of soul she had experienced; so deep were the impressions left upon her mind by the influence she had been under. I have great reason to hope she is *born again* in her old age, now upwards of fourscore. I had good hopes of the other adults, and trust they are such as God will own *in the day when He makes up His jewels.*

*June* 19.—Visited my people with two of the Reverend Correspondents. Spent time in conversation with some of them upon spiritual things, and took care of their worldly concerns.

This day makes up a complete year from the first of my preaching to these Indians in New Jersey. What amazing things has God wrought in this space of time for these poor people! What a surprising change appears in their tempers and behaviour! How are morose and savage pagans in this short space of time transformed into agreeable, affectionate, and humble Christians; and their drunken pagan howlings turned into devout and fervent prayers and praises to God! They *who were sometimes darkness are now become light in the Lord.* May they *walk as children of the light and of the day*! *And now to Him that is of power to stablish them according to the Gospel and the preaching of Christ— to God only wise be glory through Jesus Christ, for ever and ever! Amen.*

Before I conclude the present Journal, I would make a few general remarks upon what appears to me worthy of notice, relating to the continued work of grace among my people.

*First,* I cannot but notice that I have in the general, ever since my first coming among these Indians in New Jersey, been favoured with that assistance which to me is uncommon in preaching

Christ crucified, and making Him the centre and mark to which all my discourses among them were directed. It was the principal scope and drift of all my discourses to this people for several months together (after having taught them something of the being and perfections of God, His creation of man in a state of rectitude and happiness, and the obligations mankind were under to love and honour Him), to lead them into an acquaintance with their deplorable state by nature as fallen creatures; their inability to extricate and deliver themselves from it; the utter insufficiency of any external reformations and amendments of life, or of any religious performances they were capable of while in this state, to bring them into the favour of God and interest them in His eternal mercy. And thence to show them their absolute need of Christ to redeem and save them from the misery of their fallen state; to open His all-sufficiency and willingness to save the chief of sinners; the freeness and riches of His grace, proposed *without money and without price,* to all that will accept the offer; and to press them without delay to betake themselves to Him, under a sense of their misery and undone state, for relief and everlasting salvation. After this to show them the abundant encouragement the Gospel proposes to perishing and helpless sinners, in order to lead them to Christ. These things I repeatedly and largely insisted upon from time to time.

I have oftentimes remarked with admiration that, whatever subject I have been treating upon, after having spent time sufficient to explain and illustrate it, I have been naturally and easily led to Christ as the substance of all. If I treated on the being and glorious perfections of God, I was thence naturally led to discourse of Christ, as the only *way to the Father.* If I attempted to open the deplorable misery of our fallen state, it was natural from thence to show the necessity of Christ to undertake for us, to atone for our sins, and to redeem us from the power of them. If I taught the commands of God and showed our violation of them, this brought me in the most easy and natural way to speak of and recommend the Lord Jesus Christ, as One who had *magnified the law* we have broken, and who was *become the end of it for righteousness to every one that believes.* And never did I find so much freedom and assistance in making all the various lines of my discourses meet together and centre in Christ, as I have frequently done among these Indians.

Sometimes when I have had thoughts of offering but a few words upon some particular subject, and saw no occasion nor indeed much room for any considerable enlargement, there has at unawares appeared such a fountain of Gospel-grace shining forth in, or naturally resulting from, a just explication of it, and Christ has seemed in such a manner to be pointed out as the substance of what I was

considering and explaining, that I have been drawn
in a way not only easy and natural, proper and
pertinent, but almost unavoidable, to discourse of
Him either in regard of His undertaking, incarnation, satisfaction, admirable fitness for the work of
man's redemption, or the infinite need that sinners
stand in of an interest in Him. This has opened
the way for a continued strain of Gospel-invitation
to perishing souls, to come empty and naked,
weary and heavy laden, and cast themselves upon
Him.

And as I have been remarkably influenced and
assisted to dwell upon the Lord Jesus Christ and
the way of salvation by Him, in the general current
of my discourses here, and have at times been
surprisingly furnished with pertinent matter relating
to Him and the design of His incarnation; so I
have been no less assisted oftentimes in regard to
an advantageous *manner* of opening the mysteries
of divine grace, and representing the infinite ex-
cellencies and *unsearchable riches of Christ,* as well
as of recommending Him to the acceptance of
perishing sinners. I have frequently been enabled
to represent the divine glory, the infinite preciousness and transcendent loveliness of the great
Redeemer; the suitableness of His person and
purchase to supply the wants and answer the
utmost desires of immortal souls;—to open the
infinite riches of His grace, and the wonderful
encouragement proposed in the Gospel to unworthy,

helpless sinners;—to call, invite, and beseech them to come and give up themselves to Him, and be reconciled to God through Him;—to expostulate with them respecting their neglect of One so infinitely lovely and freely offered; and this in such a manner, with such freedom, pertinency, pathos, and application to the conscience, as I am sure I never could have made myself master of by the most assiduous application. I have frequently at such seasons been surprisingly helped in adapting my discourses to the capacities of my people, and bringing them down into such easy and familiar methods of expression, as has rendered them intelligible even to pagans.

I do not mention these things as a recommendation of my own performances; for I am sure I found, from time to time, that I had no skill or wisdom for my great work; and knew not how to choose out acceptable words, proper to be addressed to poor benighted pagans. But thus God was pleased to help me *not to know any thing among them, save Jesus Christ and Him crucified.* Thus I was enabled to show them their misery and undone state without Him, and to represent His complete fitness to redeem and save them. This was the preaching God made use of for the awakening of sinners, and the propagation of this "work of grace among the Indians." And it was remarkable from time to time that, when I was favoured with any special freedom in discoursing on the ability and willingness of Christ to save sinners, and the need they stood in of such a Saviour, there was then the greatest appearance of divine power in awakening numbers of secure souls, promoting convictions begun, and comforting the distressed.

I have sometimes formerly, in reading the apostle's discourse to Cornelius (Acts x.), admired to see him so quickly introduce the Lord Jesus Christ into his sermon, and so entirely dwell upon Him through the whole of it, observing him in this point very widely to differ from many of our modern preachers. But latterly this has not seemed strange, since Christ has appeared to be the substance of the Gospel, and the centre in which the several lines of divine revelation meet. Yet I am still sensible there are many things necessary to be spoken to persons under pagan darkness, in order to make way for a proper introduction of the name of Christ, and His undertaking in behalf of fallen men.

*Secondly,* It is worthy of remark that numbers of these people are brought to a strict compliance with the rules of morality and sobriety, and to a conscientious performance of the external duties of Christianity, by the internal power and influence of divine truths (the peculiar doctrines of grace) upon their minds; without their having these moral duties frequently repeated and inculcated upon them, and the contrary vices particularly exposed and spoken against. What has been the

general strain and drift of my preaching among
these Indians ; what were the truths I principally
insisted upon, and how I was influenced and
enabled to dwell from time to time upon the
peculiar doctrines of grace, I have already observed
in the preceding remark. Those doctrines which
had the most direct tendency to humble the
fallen creature ; to show him the misery of his
natural state ; to bring him down to the foot of
sovereign mercy ; to exalt the great Redeemer,
discover His transcendent excellency and infinite
preciousness, and so to recommend Him to the
sinner's acceptance, were the subject matter of
what was delivered in public and private, and
from time to time repeated and inculcated upon
them.

God was pleased to give these divine truths such
a powerful influence upon the minds of the people,
and so to bless them for the effectual awakening of numbers of them, that their lives were
quickly reformed, without my insisting upon the
precepts of morality, and spending time in repeated
harangues upon external duties. There was indeed
no room for any kind of discourses but those that
respected the essentials of religion and the experimental knowledge of divine things, whilst there
were so many enquiring daily, not how they should
regulate their external conduct (for that, persons
who are honestly disposed to comply with duty
when known, may in ordinary cases be easily

satisfied about), but how they should escape from
the wrath to come; how they might obtain an
effectual change of heart, get an interest in Christ,
and come to the enjoyment of eternal blessedness.
My great work therefore was to lead them into
a further view of their utter helplessness and the
total depravity and corruption of their hearts; that
there was no manner of goodness in them, no good
dispositions nor desires, no love to God nor delight
in His commands; but on the contrary, hatred,
enmity, and all manner of wickedness reigning in
them.   At the same time it was necessary to open
to them the glorious and complete remedy provided in Christ for helpless perishing sinners, and
offered freely to those who have no goodness of their
own, no *works of righteousness which they have done* to
recommend them to God.

This was the continued strain of my preaching,
this my great concern and constant endeavour, so
to enlighten the mind as thereby duly to affect the
heart, and as far as possible give persons a sense
and feeling of these precious and important doctrines
of grace, at least so far as means might conduce to
it.   These were the doctrines, and this the method
of preaching, which were blessed of God for the
awakening, and, I trust, for the saving conversion
of numbers of souls; and which were made the
means of producing a remarkable reformation
among the hearers in general.

When these truths were felt at heart, there was

now no vice unreformed, no external duty neglected. Drunkenness, the darling vice, was broken off, and scarcely an instance of it known among my hearers for months together. The abusive practice of husbands and wives in putting away each other, and taking others in their stead, was quickly reformed; so that there are three or four couples who have voluntarily dismissed those they had wrongfully taken, and now live together again in love and peace. The same might be said of all other vicious practices. The reformation was general; and all springing from the internal influence of divine truth upon their hearts; and not from any external restraints, or because they had heard these vices particularly exposed and repeatedly spoken against. Some of them indeed I never so much as mentioned; particularly that of the parting of men and their wives, till some, having their conscience awakened by God's Word, came, and of their own accord confessed themselves guilty in that respect. And when I did at any time mention their wicked practices, and the sins they were guilty of contrary to the light of nature, it was not with design, nor indeed with any hope, of working an effectual reformation in their external manners by this means, for I knew that while the tree remained corrupt the fruit would naturally be so; but with design to lead them, by observing the wickedness of their lives, to a view of the corruption of their hearts, and so to convince them of the necessity of a renovation of nature, and to excite them diligently to seek after that great change, which, if once obtained, would of course produce a reformation of external manners in every respect.

And as all vice was reformed upon their feeling the power of divine truth upon their hearts, so the external duties of Christianity were complied with, and conscientiously performed from the same internal influence. Family prayer was set up and constantly maintained, unless among some few more lately come, who had felt little of this divine influence. This duty constantly was performed even in some families where there were none but females, and scarce a prayerless person to be found among near a hundred of them. The Lord's day was seriously and religiously observed, and care taken by parents to keep their children orderly upon that sacred day. And this, not because I had driven them to the performance of these duties by a frequent inculcation of them, but because they had felt the power of God's Word upon their hearts ; were made sensible of their sin and misery, and thence could not but pray, and comply with everything they knew was duty, from what they felt within themselves. When their hearts were touched with a sense of their eternal concerns they could pray with great freedom as well as fervency, without being at the trouble first to learn set forms for that purpose. And some of them who were suddenly awakened at their first coming among us were brought to pray and cry for mercy with the utmost importunity, without ever being instructed in the duty of prayer, or so much as once directed to a performance of it.

The happy effects of these peculiar doctrines of grace, which I have so much insisted upon with this people, plainly discover, even to demonstration, that instead of their opening a door to licentiousness, as many vainly imagine and slanderously insinuate, they have a direct contrary tendency; so that a close application, a sense and feeling of them, will have the most powerful influence toward the renovation and effectual reformation both of heart and life.

Happy experience, as well as the Word of God and the example of Christ and His apostles, has taught me that that method of preaching which is best suited to awaken in mankind a sense and lively apprehension of their depravity and misery in a fallen state,—to excite them earnestly to seek after a change of heart, and to fly for refuge to free and sovereign grace in Christ, as the only hope set before them, is likely to be most successful toward the reformation of their external conduct. I have found that close addresses, and solemn applications of divine truth to the conscience, tend directly to strike death to the root of all vice; while smooth and plausible harangues upon moral virtues and external duties at best are likely to do no more than lop off the branches of corruption, while the root of all vice remains still untouched.

A view of the blessed effect of honest endeavours to bring home truth to the conscience, and duly to affect the heart, has often reminded me of those words of our Lord, which I have thought might be a proper exhortation for ministers in treating with others, as well as for persons in general with regard to themselves—*Cleanse first the inside of the cup and platter, that the outside may be clean also.* Cleanse, says He, the inside, *that* the outside may be clean. The only effectual way to have the outside clean is to begin with what is within; and if the fountain be purified, the streams will naturally be pure. Most certain it is, if we can awaken in sinners a lively sense of their inward pollution and depravity, their need of a change of heart, and so engage them to seek after inward cleaning; their external defilement will naturally be cleansed, their vicious ways of course be reformed, and their conversation and behaviour become regular. And though I cannot pretend that the reformation among my people does, in every instance, spring from a saving change of heart; yet I may truly say it flows from some heart-affecting view and sense of divine truth, which all have had in a greater or lesser degree.

I do not intend, by what I have observed here, to represent the preaching of morality, and pressing persons to the external performance of duty, to be altogether unnecessary and useless at any time, and especially at times when there is less of divine power attending the means of grace;—when for want of internal influences, there is need of external restraints. It is doubtless among the things that *ought to be done,* while *others are not to be left undone.* But what I principally designed by this remark was to discover plain matter of fact, namely, That the reformation, the sobriety, and external compliance with the rules and duties of Christianity, appearing among my people, are not the effect of any mere doctrinal instruction, or merely rational view of the beauty of morality, but from the internal power and influence which divine truth has had upon their hearts.

*Thirdly,* It is remarkable that God has so continued and renewed the showers of His grace here; so quickly set up His visible kingdom among these people, and so smiled upon them in relation to their acquirement of knowledge, both divine and human. It is now about a year since the beginning of this gracious out-pouring of the divine Spirit among them; and, though it has often seemed to decline and abate for some short space of time (as may be observed by several passages of my Journal, where I have endeavoured to note things just as they appeared to me from time to time); yet the shower has seemed to be renewed, and the work of grace revived again; so that a divine influence seems still apparently to attend the means of grace, in a greater or less degree, in most of our meetings for religious exercises. Religious persons are refreshed, strengthened, and established; convictions revived and promoted in many instances, and some few persons newly awakened from time to time. It must indeed be acknowledged that for some time past there has been a more manifest decline of this work, and the divine Spirit has seemed in a considerable measure withdrawn, especially in regard of His awakening influences; so that the strangers who come latterly are not seized with concern as formerly; and some few who have been much affected with divine truth in time past now appear less concerned. Yet, blessed be God, there is still an appearance of divine power and grace, a desirable degree of tenderness, religious affection, and devotion in our assemblies.

And as God has continued and renewed the showers of His grace among this people for some time; so He has with uncommon quickness set up His visible kingdom, and gathered Himself a Church in the midst of them. I have now baptized, since the conclusion of my last Journal, thirty persons, fifteen adults and fifteen children. These, added to the number there mentioned, make seventy-seven persons; thirty-eight adults and thirty-nine children; and all within the space of eleven months past. And it must be noted that I have baptized no adults but such as appeared to have a work of special grace wrought in their hearts; I mean such who have had the experience not only of the awakening and humbling, but, in a judgment of charity, of the renewing and comforting influences of the divine Spirit. There are also many others under solemn concern for their souls, who I apprehend are persons of sufficient knowledge and visible seriousness, to render them proper subjects of the ordinance of baptism. Yet since they give no comfortable evidence of having as yet passed a saving change, but only appear under conviction of sin and misery, and, having no principle of spiritual life wrought in them, are liable to lose the impressions of religion they are now under; and considering the great propensity there is in this people naturally to abuse themselves with strong drink, and fearing lest some, who at present appear serious and concerned for their souls, might lose their concern and return to this sin, and so, if baptized, prove a scandal to their profession; I have thought proper hitherto to omit the baptism of any but such as give some hopeful evidence of a saving change, although I do not pretend to determine positively respecting the state of any.

I likewise administered the Lord's Supper to a number of persons, who I have abundant reason to think (as I elsewhere observed) were proper subjects of that ordinance, within the space of ten months and ten days after my first coming among these Indians in New Jersey. And from the time that, I am informed, some of them were attending an idolatrous feast and sacrifice in honour of devils, to the time they sat down at the Lord's Table (I trust) to the honour of God, was not more than a full year. Surely Christ's little flock here, so suddenly gathered from among pagans, may justly say, in the language of the Church of old, *The Lord hath done great things for us whereof we are glad.*

Much of the goodness of God has also appeared in their acquirement of knowledge, both in religion and in the affairs of common life. There has been a wonderful thirst after Christian knowledge prevailing among them in general, and an eager desire of being instructed in Christian doctrines and manners. This has prompted them to ask many pertinent as well as important questions; the answers to which have tended much to enlighten their minds and promote their knowledge in divine things. Many of the doctrines I have delivered they queried with me about, in order to gain further insight into them; and have from time to time manifested a good understanding of them, by their answers to the questions proposed to them in my Catechetical lectures. They have likewise queried with me respecting a proper method as well as proper matter of prayer, and expressions suitable to be made use of in that religious exercise; and have taken pains in order to the performance of this duty with understanding. They have also taken pains and appeared remarkably apt in learning to sing Psalm tunes, and are now able to sing with a good degree of decency in the worship of God.

They have also acquired a considerable degree of useful knowledge in the affairs of common life. They now appear like rational creatures, fit for human society, free from that savage roughness and brutish stupidity, which rendered them very disagreeable in their pagan state. They seem ambitious of a thorough acquaintance with the English language, and for that end frequently speak it among themselves. Many of them have made good proficiency in it, since my coming among them. Indeed most of them can understand a considerable part, and some the substance of my discourses, without an interpreter; being used to my low and familiar methods of expression, though they could not well understand other ministers.

And as they are desirous of instruction and surprisingly apt in receiving it, so divine Providence has afforded them the proper means for this purpose. The attempts made to raise a school among them have been succeeded, and a kind Providence has sent them a schoolmaster, of whom I may justly say, I know of *no man like minded who will naturally care for their state.* He has generally thirty or thirty-five children in his school; and when he kept an evening school, as he did while the length of the evenings would admit of it, he had fifteen or twenty people, married and single.

The children learn with surprising readiness; their master tells me, he never had an English school that learned in general so fast. There were not above two in thirty, although some of them were very small, but what learned to know all the letters in the alphabet distinctly, within three days after his entrance upon his business, while several in that space of time learned to spell considerably. Some of them, since the beginning of February last, at which time the school was set up, have learned so much that they are able to read in a Psalter or Testament without spelling.

They are instructed twice a week in the Assembly's Shorter Catechism, on Wednesday and Saturday. Some of them, since the latter end of February, at which time they began, have learned to say it pretty distinctly by heart, considerably more than half through; and most of them have made some proficiency in it. They are likewise instructed in the duty of secret prayer, and most of them constantly attend it night and morning, and are very careful to inform their master if they apprehend any of their little schoolmates neglect that holy exercise.

*Fourthly,* It is worthy to be noted, to the praise of sovereign grace, that amidst so great a work of conviction, so much concern and religious affection, there has been no prevalency, nor indeed any considerable appearance of false religion, if I may so term it; or heats of imagination, intemperate zeal, and spiritual pride. These corrupt mixtures too often attend the revival and powerful propagation of religion; but in the present instance there has been very little irregular or scandalous behaviour among those who have appeared serious. I may justly repeat what I observed at the conclusion of my last Journal,—that there has here been no appearance of " bodily agonies, convulsions, frightful screamings, swoonings," and the like. I may now further add that there has been no prevalency of visions, trances, and imaginations of any kind; though there has been an appearance of something of that nature since the conclusion of that Journal. An instance of this sort I have given an account of in my Journal of December 26.

This work of grace has in the main been carried on with a surprising degree of purity, and freedom from corrupt mixture. The religious concern that persons have been under has generally been rational and just; arising from a sense of their sins, and exposedness to the divine displeasure on account of them; as well as their utter inability to deliver themselves from the misery they felt and feared. If there has been in any instance an appearance of irrational concern and perturbation of mind, when the subjects of it knew not why, yet there has been no prevalency of any such thing; and indeed I scarcely know of any instance of that nature at all. And it is very remarkable that, although the concern of many persons under convictions of their perishing state has been very great and pressing, yet I have never seen anything like desperation attending it in any one instance. They have had the most lively sense of their undone state; have been brought to give up all hopes of deliverance from themselves, while their spiritual exercises have been attended with great distress and anguish of soul. Yet in the seasons of the greatest extremity there has been no appearance of despair in any of them,—nothing that has discouraged or in any wise hindered them from the most diligent use of all proper means for their conversion and salvation. Hence it is apparent there is not that danger of persons being driven into despair under spiritual trouble, unless in cases of deep and habitual melancholy, that the world in general is ready to imagine.

The comfort that persons have obtained after their distresses has likewise in general appeared solid, well-grounded, and scriptural; arising from a spiritual and supernatural illumination of mind,— a view of divine things in a measure *as they are*, a complacency of soul in the divine perfections, and a peculiar satisfaction in the way of salvation by the great Redeemer. Their joys seemed to rise from a variety of views and considerations of divine things, although for substance the same. Some, who under conviction seemed to have the hardest struggles and heart-risings against divine sovereignty, have seemed at the first dawn of their comfort to rejoice in a peculiar manner in that divine perfection,—have been delighted to think that themselves, and all things else, were in the hand of God, and that He would dispose of them just as He pleased. Others, who just before their reception of comfort, have been remarkably oppressed with a sense of their helplessness and poverty, who have seen themselves as it were falling down into remediless perdition, have been at first more peculiarly delighted with a view of the freeness and riches of divine grace, and the offer of salvation to perishing sinners *without money and without price*.

Some have at first appeared to rejoice especially in the wisdom of God, discovered in the way of salvation by Christ. It appeared to them *a new and living way*, a way they had never had any just conception of, until opened to them by the special influence of the divine Spirit. Some of them, upon a lively spiritual view of this way of salvation, have wondered at their past folly in seeking salvation in any other way, and that they never saw this way of salvation before, which now appeared so plain and easy, as well as excellent to them. Others again have had a more general view of the beauty and excellency of Christ, and have had their souls delighted with an apprehension of His divine glory, as unspeakably exceeding all they had ever conceived before; yet without singling out, as it were, any one of the divine perfections in particular: so that, although their comfort seemed to arise from a variety of views and considerations of the divine glories, still they were spiritual and supernatural views of them, and not groundless fancies, that were the spring of their joys and comforts.

It must be acknowledged, however, that, when this work became so universal and prevalent, and gained such general credit and esteem among the Indians, that Satan seemed to have little advantage of working against it in his own proper garb, he then transformed himself *into an angel of light,* and made some vigorous attempts to introduce turbulent commotions of the passions in the room of genuine convictions of sin, imaginary and fanciful notions of Christ, as appearing to the mental eye in a human shape, and being in some particular postures, instead of spiritual and supernatural discoveries of His divine glory and excellency. If these and similar delusions had met with countenance and encouragement, there would have been a very considerable harvest of this kind of converts here. Spiritual pride also discovered itself in various instances. Some persons who had been under great affections seemed desirous of being thought truly gracious; who, when I could not but express to them my fears respecting their spiritual state, discovered their resentment to a considerable degree upon that occasion. There also appeared in one or two of them an unbecoming ambition of being teachers of others. So that Satan has been a busy adversary here as well as elsewhere. But blessed be God, though something of this nature has appeared, yet nothing of it has prevailed nor indeed made any considerable progress. My people are now apprised of these things, are acquainted that Satan in such a manner *transformed himself into an angel of light,* in the first season of the great out-pouring of the divine Spirit in the days of the apostles; and that something of this nature, in a greater or lesser degree, has attended almost every revival and remarkable propagation of true religion ever since. And they have learned so to distinguish between the gold and the dross, that the credit of the latter is *trod down like the mire of the streets* ; and it being natural for this kind of stuff to die with its credit, there is now scarcely any appearance of it among them.

And as there has been no prevalency of irregular heats, imaginary notions, spiritual pride, and Satanical delusions among my people; so there have been a very few instances of scandalous and irregular behaviour among those who have made a profession or even an appearance of seriousness. I do not know of more than three or four such persons that have been guilty of any open mis-conduct, since their first acquaintance with Christianity, and not one that persists in anything of that nature. Perhaps the remarkable purity of this work in the latter respect, its freedom from frequent instances of scandal, is very much owing to its purity in the former respects, its freedom from corrupt mixtures of spiritual pride, wild-fire, and delusion, which naturally lay a foundation for scandalous practices.

May this blessed work in the power and purity of it prevail among the poor Indians here, as well as spread elsewhere, till their remotest tribes shall see the salvation of God! Amen.        D. B.

# FIRST APPENDIX TO THE
# JOURNAL.

I should have concluded what I had at present to offer respecting my mission, but that I lately received, from the President of the Correspondents, the copy of a letter directed to him from the Society for Propagating Christian Knowledge, dated at Edinburgh, March 21, 1745, expressly enjoining upon their missionaries : "That they give an exact account of the methods they make use of for instructing themselves in the Indian language, and what progress they have already made in it. What methods they are now taking to instruct the Indians in the principles of our holy religion; and particularly, that they set forth in their Journals what difficulties they have already met with, and the methods they make use of for surmounting the same."

As to the two former of these particulars, I trust that what I have already noted in my Journals from time to time might have been in a good measure satisfactory to the Honourable Society, had these Journals arrived safely and seasonably, which I am sensible they have not in general done, by reason of their falling into the hands of the enemy, although I have been at the pains of sending two copies of every Journal for more than two years past, lest one might miscarry in the passage. But with relation to the latter of these particulars, I have purposely omitted saying anything consider- able, and that for these two reasons. *First,* Because I could not oftentimes give any tolerable account of the difficulties I met with in my work, without speaking somewhat particularly of the causes of them and the circumstances conducing to them, which would necessarily have rendered my Journals very lengthy and tedious. Besides, some of the causes of my difficulties I thought more fit to be concealed than divulged. *Secondly,* Because I thought a frequent mentioning of the difficulties attending my work might appear as an unbecoming complaint under my burdens; or as if I would rather be thought to be endowed with a singular measure of self-denial, constancy, and holy resolution, to meet and confront so many difficulties, and yet to hold on and go forward amidst them all. But since the Honourable Society are pleased to require a more exact and particular account of these things, I shall cheerfully endeavour something for their satisfaction in relation to each of these particulars; although in regard of the latter, I am ready to say, *Infandum jubes renovare dolorem.*

The most successful method I have taken for

instructing myself in any of the Indian languages is, to translate English discourses by the help of an interpreter or two into their language, as nearly *verbatim* as the sense will admit, and to observe strictly how they use words, and what construction they will bear in various cases; and thus to gain some acquaintance with the root from whence particular words proceed, and to see how they are thence varied and diversified. But here occurs a very great difficulty; for the interpreters being unlearned and unacquainted with the rules of language, it is impossible sometimes to know by them the part of speech of some particular words, whether noun, verb, or participle; for they seem to use participles sometimes where we should use nouns, and sometimes where we should use verbs in the English language. But notwithstanding many difficulties, I have gained some acquaintance with the grounds of the Delaware language, and have learned most of the defects in it; so that I know what English words can, and what cannot be translated into it. I have also gained some acquaintance with the particular phraseologies, as well as peculiarities of their language, one of which I cannot but mention. Their language does not admit of their speaking any word denoting relation, such as father, son, *absolutely*; that is, without prefixing a pronoun passive to it, such as my, thy, his. Hence they cannot be baptized in their own language in the name of *the* Father, and *the* Son;

but they may be baptized in the name of Jesus Christ and *His* Father. I have gained so much knowledge of their language that I can understand a considerable part of what they say, when they discourse upon divine things, and am frequently able to correct my interpreter, if he mistakes my meaning. But I can do nothing to any purpose at speaking the language myself.

As an apology for this defect, I must renew, or rather enlarge my former complaint, That "while so much of my time is necessarily consumed in journeying," while I am obliged to ride four thousand miles a year, as I have done in the year past, "I can have little left for any of my necessary studies, and consequently for the study of the Indian languages." This I may venture to say is the great, if not the only, reason why the Delaware language is not familiar to me before this time; and it is impossible I should ever be able to speak it without close application, which at present I see no prospect of having time for. To preach and catechise frequently; to converse privately with persons that need so much instruction and direction as these poor Indians do; to take care of all their secular affairs, as if they were a company of children; to ride abroad frequently in order to procure collections for the support of the school, and for their help and benefit in other respects; to hear and decide all the petty differences that arise among any of them, and to have the constant oversight and management of all their affairs of every kind, must needs engross most of my time, and leave me little for application to the study of the Indian languages. And when I add to this the time that is necessarily consumed upon my Journals, I must say I have little to spare for other business. As was observed before, I have not sent to the Honourable Society less than two copies of every Journal for more than two years past, most of which, I suppose, have been taken by the French in their passage. A third copy I have constantly kept by me, lest the others should miscarry. This has caused me not a little labour, and so straitened me for time, when I have been at liberty from other business, and had opportunity to sit down to writing, which is but rare, that I have been obliged to write twelve and thirteen hours in a day, till my spirits have been extremely wasted and my life almost spent, to get these writings accomplished. And, after all, after diligent application to the various parts of my work, and after the most industrious improvement of time I am capable of, both early and late, I cannot oftentimes possibly gain two hours in a week for reading or any other studies, unless just for what urges and appears of absolute necessity for the present. Frequently when I attempt to redeem time, by sparing it out of my sleeping hours, I am by that means thrown under bodily indisposition and rendered fit for nothing.

This is truly my present state, and is likely to be

so, for aught I can see, unless I could procure an assistant in my work or quit my present business. But though I have not made that proficiency I could wish in learning the Indian languages, yet I have used all endeavours to instruct them in the English tongue, which perhaps will be more advantageous to the Christian interest among them than if I should preach in their own language, for that is very defective, as I shall hereafter observe ; so that many things cannot be communicated to them without introducing English terms.   Besides, they can have no books translated into their language, without great difficulty and expense ; and, if still accustomed to their own language only, they would have no advantage of hearing other ministers occasionally or in my absence.   If therefore I had a perfect acquaintance with the Indian language, it would be of no great importance with regard to the congregation of Indians in New Jersey, though it might be of service to me in treating with the Indians elsewhere.

The methods I am taking to instruct the Indians in the principles of our holy religion are, to preach, or open and improve some particular points of doctrine ; to expound particular paragraphs, or sometimes whole chapters of God's Word to them ; to give historical relations from Scripture of the most material and remarkable occurrences relating to the Church of God from the beginning ; and frequently to catechise them upon the principles of

Christianity. The latter of these methods of instructing I manage in a twofold manner. I sometimes catechise systematically, proposing questions agreeable to the Assembly's Shorter Catechism This I have carried on to a considerable length. At other times I catechise upon any important subject that I think difficult to them. Sometimes when I have discoursed upon some particular point, and made it as plain and familiar to them as I can, I then catechise upon the most material branches of my discourse, to see whether they had a thorough understanding of it. But as I have catechised chiefly in a systematic form, I shall here give some specimen of the method I make use of, as well as of the propriety and justness of my people's answers to the questions proposed to them.

### QUESTIONS UPON THE BENEFITS BELIEVERS RECEIVE FROM CHRIST AT DEATH.

*Q.* I have shown you that the children of God receive a great many good things from Christ while they live ; now have they any more to receive when they come to die ?

*A.* Yes.

*Q.* Are the children of God then made perfectly free from sin ?

*A* Yes.

*Q.* Do you think they will never more be troubled with vain, foolish, and wicked thoughts ?

*A.* No, never at all.

*Q.* Will not they then be like the good angels I have so often told you of?

*A.* Yes.

*Q.* And do you call *this* a great measure to be freed from all sin?

*A.* Yes.

*Q.* Do all God's children count it so?

*A.* Yes, all of them.

*Q.* Do you think this is what they would ask for above all things, if God should say to them, Ask what you will, and it shall be done for you?

*A.* O yes, be sure, that is what they want.

*Q.* You say the souls of God's people at death are made perfectly free from sin; where do they go then?

*A.* They go and live with Jesus Christ.

*Q.* Does Christ show them more respect and honour, and make them more happy [1] than we can possibly think of in this world?

*A.* Yes.

*Q.* Do they go *immediately* to live with Christ in heaven as soon as their bodies are dead; or do they tarry somewhere else a while?

*A.* They go immediately to Christ.

*Q.* Does Christ take any care of the bodies of His

[1] The only way I have to express their "entering into glory," or being glorified; there being no word in the Indian language answering to that general term.

people when they are dead, and their souls gone to heaven, or does He forget them?

*A.* He takes care of them.

These questions were all answered with surprising readiness, and without once missing, as I remember. And in answering several of them which respected deliverance from sin, they were much affected and melted with the hopes of that happy state.

QUESTIONS UPON THE BENEFITS BELIEVERS RECEIVE FROM CHRIST AT THE RESURRECTION.

*Q.* You see I have already shown you what good things Christ gives His good people while they live, and when they come to die; now, will He raise their bodies, and the bodies of others, to life again at the last day?

*A.* Yes, they shall all be raised.

*Q.* Shall they then have the same bodies they now have?

*A.* Yes.

*Q.* Will their bodies then be weak, will they feel cold, hunger, thirst, and weariness, as they now do?

*A.* No, none of these things.

*Q.* Will their bodies ever die any more after they are raised to life?

*A.* No.

*Q.* Will their souls and bodies be joined together again?

*A.* Yes.

*Q.* Will God's people be more happy then, than they were while their bodies were asleep?

*A.* Yes.

*Q.* Will Christ then own these to be His people before all the world?

*A.* Yes.

*Q.* But God's people find so much sin in themselves, that they are often ashamed of themselves, and will not Christ be ashamed to own such for His friends at that day?

*A.* No, He will never be ashamed of them.

*Q.* Will Christ then show all the world, that He has put away these people's sins;[1] and that He looks upon them as if they had never sinned at all?

*A.* Yes.

*Q.* Will He look upon them as if they had never sinned, for the sake of any good things they have done themselves, or for the sake of His righteousness accounted to them as if it was theirs?

*A.* For the sake of His righteousness counted to them, not for their own goodness.

*Q.* Will God's children then be as happy as they can desire to be?

*A.* Yes.

---

[1] The only way I have to express their being openly acquitted. When I speak of justification, I have no other way but to call it God's looking upon us as good creatures.

*Q.* The children of God, while in this world, can but now and then draw near unto Him, and they are ready to think they can never have enough of God in Christ; but will they have enough there, as much as they can desire?

*A.* O yes, enough, enough.

*Q.* Will the children of God love Him then as much as they desire; will they find nothing to hinder their love from going to Him?

*A.* Nothing at all; they shall love Him as much as they desire.

*Q.* Will they never be weary of God and Christ, and the pleasures of heaven, so as we are weary of our friends and enjoyments here, after we have been pleased with them a-while?

*A.* No, never.

*Q.* Could God's people be happy if they knew God loved them, and yet felt at the same time that they could not love and honour Him?

*A.* No, no.

*Q.* Will this then make God's people perfectly happy, to love God above all, to honour Him continually, and to feel His love to them?

*A.* Yes.

*Q.* And will this happiness last for ever?

*A.* Yes, for ever, for ever!

These questions, like the former, were answered without hesitation or missing, as I remember, in any one instance.

QUESTIONS UPON THE DUTY WHICH GOD REQUIRES
OF MAN.

*Q.* Has God let us know anything of His will,
or what He would have us do to please Him?

*A.* Yes.

*Q.* And does He require us to do His will, and
to please Him?

*A.* Yes.

*Q.* Is it right that God should require this of us;
has He any business to command us as a father
does his children?

*A.* Yes.

*Q.* Why is it right that God should command us
to do what He pleases?

*A.* Because He made us, and gives us all our
good things.

*Q.* Does God require us to do anything that
will hurt us, and take away our comfort and
happiness?

*A.* No.

*Q.* But God requires sinners to repent and be
sorry for their sins, and to have their hearts
broken; now, does not this hurt them, and take
away their comfort, to be made sorry, and to have
their hearts broken?

*A.* No, it does them good.

*Q.* Did God teach man His will at first by writing it down in a book, or did He put it into his

heart, and teach him without a book what was right?

*A.* He put it into his heart, and made him know what he should do.

*Q.* Has God since that time written down His will in a book?

*A.* Yes.

*Q.* Has God written His whole will in His book; has He there told us all that He would have us believe and do?

*A.* Yes.

*Q.* What need was there of this book, if God at first put His will into the heart of man, and made him feel what he should do?

*A.* There was need of it, because we have sinned and made our hearts blind.

*Q.* And has God written down the same things in His book, that He at first put into the heart of man?

*A.* Yes.

In this manner I endeavour to adapt my instructions to the capacities of the people; although they may perhaps seem strange to others who have never experienced the difficulty of the work. It is my great concern, I trust, that instruction be given them in such a manner, that they may not only be doctrinally taught, but duly affected thereby; that divine truth may come to them, *not in word only, but also in power, and in the Holy Ghost, and in much assurance.*

DIFFICULTIES IN EVANGELISING THE INDIANS.

I shall now attempt something with regard to the last particular required by the Honourable Society in their letter, namely, To give some account of the " difficulties I have already met with in my work, and the methods I make use of for surmounting the same." What I have to say upon this subject, I shall reduce to the following heads :

*First,* I have met with great difficulty in my work among the Indians, *from the rooted aversion to Christianity that generally prevails among them.* They are not only brutishly stupid and ignorant of divine things, but many of them are obstinately set against Christianity, and seem to abhor even the Christian name.

This aversion arises partly from a view of the *immorality and vicious behaviour of many who are called Christians.* They observe that horrid wickedness in nominal Christians which the light of nature condemns in themselves; and not having distinguishing views of things, they are ready to look upon all the white people alike, and to condemn them alike for the abominable practices of some. Hence, when I have attempted to treat with them about Christianity, they have frequently objected the scandalous practices of Christians, and cast in my teeth all they could think of that was odious in the conduct of any of them. They have observed to me that the white people lie, defraud, steal, and drink, worse than the Indians; that they have taught the Indians these things, especially the latter of them; who before the coming of the English knew of no such thing as strong drink; that the English have by these means made them quarrel and kill one another; and in a word, brought them to the practice of all those vices which now prevail among them. So that they are now more vicious, and much more miserable, than they were before the coming of the white people into the country.

These, and such like objections, they frequently make against Christianity, which are not easily answered to their satisfaction; many of them being facts too notoriously true. The only way I have to take in order to surmount this difficulty is to distinguish between nominal and real Christians; and to show them that the ill conduct of many of the former proceeds not from their being Christians, but from their being Christians only in name and not in heart. To this it has sometimes been objected that, if all those who will cheat the Indians are Christians only in name, there are but few left in the country to be Christians in heart. This and many other of the remarks they pass upon the white people, and their miscarriages, I am forced to own, and cannot but grant that many nominal Christians are more abominably wicked than the Indians. But then I attempt to show them, that there are some who feel the power of Christianity who are not so. And I ask them, when they ever saw me guilty of the vices they complain of, and charge Christians in general with? Still the great difficulty is that the people who live back in the country nearest to them, and the traders that go among them, are generally of the most irreligious and vicious sort; and the conduct of one or two persons, however exemplary, is not sufficient to counterbalance the vicious behaviour of so many of the same denomination, and so to recommend Christianity to pagans.

Another thing that serves to make them more averse to Christianity is *a fear of being enslaved.* They are perhaps some of the most jealous people living, and extremely averse to a state of servitude; hence they are always afraid of some design forming against them. Besides, they seem to have no sentiments of generosity, benevolence, and goodness; so that, if anything be proposed to them for their good, they are ready rather to suspect that there is at bottom some design forming against them, than that such proposals flow from good-will to them and a desire of their welfare. Hence, when I have attempted to recommend Christianity to their acceptance, they have sometimes objected that the white people have come among them, have cheated them out of their lands, driven them back to the mountains from the pleasant places they used to enjoy by the sea-side; that therefore they have no reason to think the white people are now seeking their welfare; but rather that they have sent me out to draw them together, under a pretence of kindness to them, that they may have an opportunity to make slaves of them, as they do of the poor negroes, or else to ship them on board their vessels and make them fight with their enemies. Thus they have oftentimes construed all the kindness I could show them, and the hardships I have endured in order to treat with them about Christianity. "He never would (say they) take all the pains to do us good; he must have some wicked design to hurt us some way or other." To give them assurance of the contrary is not an easy matter, while there are so many who, according to their apprehension, are only *seeking their own*, not the good of others.

To remove this difficulty I inform them that I am not sent out by those persons in these provinces, who they suppose have cheated them out of their lands, but by pious people at a great distance, who never had an inch of their lands, nor ever thought of doing them any hurt; but here will arise so many frivolous and impertinent questions, that it would tire one's patience and wear out one's spirits to hear them. They would say, "But why did not these good people send you to teach us *before*, while we had our lands down by the sea-side? If they had sent you then, we should likely have heard you and become Christians." The poor creatures still imagining that I should be much beholden to them, in case they would hearken to Christianity ; and insinuating that this was a favour they could not now be so good as to show me, seeing they had received so many injuries from the white people.

Another spring of aversion to Christianity in the Indians is *their strong attachment to their own religious notions*, if they may be called religious, and the early prejudices they have imbibed in favour of their own frantic and ridiculous kind of worship. What their notions of God are in their pagan state, it is difficult precisely to determine.    I have taken much pains to enquire of my Christian people whether, before their acquaintance with Christianity, they imagined there was a plurality of great invisible powers, or whether they supposed but one such being and worshipped him in a variety of forms and shapes ; but I cannot learn anything of them so as to be fully satisfied upon the point. Their notions in that state were so prodigiously dark and confused, that they seemed not to know what they thought themselves.    But, so far as I can learn, they had a notion of a plurality of invisible deities, and paid some kind of homage to them promiscuously, under a great variety of forms and shapes.    It is certain that those who yet remain pagans pay some kind of superstitious reverence to beasts, birds, fishes, and even reptiles ; that is, some to one kind of animal, and some to another.

They do not indeed suppose a divine power essential to, or inhering in, these creatures, but that some invisible beings, not distinguished from each other by certain names, but only notionally, communicate to these animals a great power, either one or other of them, just as it happens, or perhaps sometimes all of them, and so make these creatures the immediate authors of good to certain persons. Hence such a creature becomes sacred to the persons to whom he is supposed to be the immediate author of good, and through him they must worship the invisible powers, though to others he is no more than another creature. Another animal perhaps is looked upon to be the immediate author of good to another person, and consequently he must worship the invisible powers in that animal. And I have known a pagan burn fine tobacco for incense, in order to appease the anger of that invisible power which he supposed presided over rattlesnakes, because one of these animals was killed by another Indian near his house.

After the strictest enquiry respecting their notions of the Deity, I find that in ancient times, before the coming of the white people, some supposed there were four invisible powers who presided over the four corners of the earth. Others imagined the sun to be the only deity, and that all things were made by him; others at the same time having a confused notion of a certain body or fountain of deity, somewhat like the *anima mundi*, so frequently mentioned by the more learned ancient heathen, diffusing itself to various animals and even to inanimate things, making them the immediate authors of good to certain persons, as was before observed, with respect to various supposed deities. But after the coming of the white people, they seemed to suppose there were three deities, and three only, because they saw people of three different kinds of complexion,—English, Negroes, and themselves.

It is a notion pretty generally prevailing among them, that it was not the same God made them who made us; but that they were made after the white people; which further shows that they imagine a plurality of divine powers. And I fancy they suppose their God gained some special skill by seeing the white people made, and so made *them* better; for it is certain they look upon themselves and their methods of living, which they say their God expressly prescribed for them, as greatly preferable to the white people and their methods. Hence they will frequently sit and laugh at them, as being good for nothing else but to plough and fatigue themselves with hard labour; while *they* enjoy the satisfaction of stretching themselves on the ground, and sleeping as much as they please; and have no other trouble but now and then to chase the deer, which is often attended with pleasure rather than pain. Hence also many of them look upon it as disgraceful for them to become Christians, as it would be esteemed among Christians for any to become pagans.  But though they suppose our religion will do well enough for us, because prescribed by *our* God, yet it is no ways proper for them, because not of the same make and original.  This they have sometimes offered as a reason why they did not incline to hearken to Christianity.

They seem to have some confused notion about a future state of existence, and many of them imagine that the *chichuny*, the shadow, or what survives the body, will at death go southward, and in an unknown but curious place will enjoy some kind of happiness, such as hunting, feasting, dancing, and the like.  And what they suppose will contribute much to their happiness in that state is that they shall never be weary of those entertainments.  It seems by this notion of their going southward to obtain happiness, as if they had their course into these parts of the world from some very cold climate, and found the farther they went southward the more comfortable they were; and thence concluded that perfect felicity was to be found farther towards the same point.

They appear to entertain some faint and glimmering notion about rewards and punishments, or at least happiness and misery in a future state, that is, some that I have conversed with, though others seem to know of no such thing.  Those who suppose this seem to imagine that most will be happy, and that those who are not so will be punished only with privation, being only excluded the walls of that good world where happy souls shall dwell. These rewards and punishments they suppose to depend entirely upon their conduct, as to the duties of the second table, that is, their behaviour towards mankind, and seem, so far as I can see, not to imagine that they have any reference to their *religious* notions or practices, or anything that relates to the worship of God. I remember I once consulted a very ancient but intelligent Indian upon this point, for my own satisfaction. I asked him whether the Indians of old times supposed there was anything of the man that would survive the body. He replied, Yes. I asked him where they supposed its abode would be. He replied, " It would go southward." I asked him further, whether it would be happy there. He answered, after a considerable pause, " that the souls of good folks would be happy, and the souls of bad folks miserable." I then asked him, who he called bad folks. His answer was, " Those who lie, steal, quarrel with their neighbours, are unkind to their friends, and especially to aged parents, and, in a word, such as are a plague to mankind." These were his " bad folks " ; but not a word was said about their neglect of divine worship, and their badness in that respect.

They have indeed some kind of religious worship, are frequently offering sacrifices to some supposed invisible powers, and are very ready to impute their calamities in the present world to the neglect of these sacrifices; but there is no appearance of reverence or devotion in the homage they pay them; and what they do of this nature seems to be done only to appease the supposed anger of their deities, to engage them to be placable to themselves and do them no hurt; or at most, only to invite these powers to succeed them in those enterprises they are engaged in respecting the present life. In offering these sacrifices they seem to have no reference to a future state, but only to present comfort; and this is the account my interpreter always gives me of this matter. "They sacrifice," says he, "that they may have success in hunting and other affairs, and that sickness and other calamities may not befal them, which they fear in the present world in case of neglect; but they do not suppose God will ever punish them in the coming world for neglecting to sacrifice." Indeed they seem to imagine that those whom they call "bad folks" are excluded from the company of good people in that state, not so much because God remembers and is determined to punish them for sin of any kind, either immediately against Himself or their neighbour, as because they would be a "plague" to society, and would render others unhappy if admitted to dwell with them. So that they are excluded rather of necessity than by the act of a righteous Judge.

The Indians give much heed to *dreams,* because they suppose these invisible powers to give them directions at such times about certain affairs, and inform them what animal they would choose to be worshipped in. They are likewise much attached to the traditions and fabulous notions of their fathers, who have informed them of divers miracles that were anciently wrought among the Indians, which they firmly believe, and thence look upon their ancestors to have been the best of men. They also mention some wonderful things which, they say, have happened since the memory of some who are now living. One affirmed to me that he himself had once been dead four days; that most of his friends were gathered together to his funeral, and that he should have been buried, but that some of his relations at a great distance, who were sent for upon that occasion, were not arrived; and before their coming he came to life again. During this time, he says, he went to the place where the sun rises (imagining the earth to be plain), and directly over that place, at a great height in the air, he was admitted into a great house, which he supposes was several miles in length, and saw many wonderful things, too tedious as well as ridiculous to mention. Another person, a woman, whom I have not seen but have been credibly informed of by the Indians, declares that she was dead several days; that her soul went southward, and feasted and danced with the happy spirits; and that she found all things exactly agreeable to the Indian notions of a future state.

To these superstitious notions and traditions, and this kind of ridiculous worship, the Indians are extremely attached; and the prejudice they have imbibed in favour of these things renders them not a little averse to the doctrines of Christianity. Hence some of them have told me, when I have endeavoured to instruct them, "that their fathers had taught them already, and that they did not want to learn now."

It will be too tedious to give any considerable account of the methods I make use of for surmounting this difficulty. I will just say that I endeavour as much as possible to show them the inconsistency of their own notions, and so to confound them out of their own mouths. But I must also say, I have sometimes been almost nonplussed with them, and scarcely knew what to answer them; but never have been more perplexed than when they have pretended to yield to me as knowing more than they, and consequently have asked me numbers of impertinent and yet difficult questions; such as, " How the Indians came first into this part of the world, away from all the white people, if what I said was true,—that the same God made them who made us ? " " How the Indians became black, if they had the same original parents with the white people ? "

What further contributes to their aversion to

Christianity is *the influence that their Powwows, conjurers or diviners, have upon them.* These persons are supposed to have a power of foretelling future events, of recovering the sick at least oftentimes, and of charming, enchanting, or poisoning persons to death by their magic divinations. Their spirit, in its various operations, seems to be a Satanical imitation of the spirit of prophecy which the Church in early ages enjoyed. Some of these diviners are endowed with this spirit in infancy; others in adult age. It seems not to depend upon their own will, nor to be acquired by any endeavours of the person who is the subject of it, though it is supposed to be given to children sometimes in consequence of some means which the parents use with them for that purpose. One of these is, to make the child swallow a small living frog, after having performed some superstitious rites and ceremonies upon it. They are not under the influence of this spirit always alike, but it comes upon them at times; and those who are endowed with it are accounted singularly favoured.

I have laboured to gain some information respecting their conjuration, and have for that end consulted with the man mentioned in my Journal of May 9, who, since his conversion to Christianity, has endeavoured to give me the best intelligence he could of this matter. But it seems to be such a *mystery of iniquity,* that I cannot well understand it, and know not oftentimes what ideas to affix to the terms he makes use of; and so far as I can learn, he himself has not any clear notions of the thing, now his spirit of divination is gone from him. However, the manner in which he says he obtained this spirit of divination was this : he was admitted into the presence of a great man, who informed him that he loved, pitied, and desired to do him good. It was not in this world that he saw the great man, but in a world above at a vast distance from this. The great man, he says, was clothed with the day; yea, with the brightest day he ever saw; a day of many years, yea, of everlasting continuance. This whole world, he says, was drawn upon him, so that *in* him the earth and all things in it might be seen. I asked him if rocks, mountains, and seas were drawn upon or appeared in him. He replied, every thing that was beautiful and lovely in the earth was upon him, and might be seen by looking on him, as well as if one was on the earth to take a view of him there. By the side of the great man, he says, stood his shadow or spirit; for he used *chichuny,* the word they commonly make use of to express that of the man which survives the body, which word properly signifies a shadow. This shadow, he says, was as lovely as the man himself, and filled all places, and was most agreeable as well as wonderful to him. Here, he says, he tarried some time, and was un-speakably entertained and delighted with a view of the great man, of his shadow or spirit, and of all things in him. And what is most of all astonishing, he imagines all this to have passed before he was born. He never had been, he says, in this world at that time. And what confirms him in the belief of this is, that the great man told him that he must come down to earth, be born of such a woman, meet with such and such things, and in particular, that he should once in this life be guilty of murder. At this he was displeased, and told the great man he would never murder. But the great man replied, " I have said it, and it shall be so " ; and it accordingly happened. At this time, he says, the great man asked him what he would choose in life. He replied, first to be a hunter, and afterwards to be a Powwow or diviner. The great man told him he should have what he desired, and that his shadow should go along with him down to earth, and be with him for ever. There was, he says, all this time, no word spoken between them. The conference was not carried on by any human language, but they had a kind of mental intelligence of each other's thoughts, dispositions, and proposals. After this he saw the great man no more ; but supposes he now came down to earth to be born. The spirit or shadow of the great man still attended him, and ever after continued to appear to him in dreams and other ways, until he felt the power of God's Word upon his heart ; since which it has entirely left him.

This spirit, he says, used sometimes to direct

him in dreams to go to such a place and hunt, assuring him he should there meet with success, and so it proved. When he had been there some time, the spirit would order him to another place. Thus he had success in hunting, according to the great man's promise made to him at the time of his choosing this employment.

Sometimes this spirit came upon him in a special manner, and he was full of what he saw in the great man. Then he says he was all light, and not only light himself, but it was light all around him, so that he could see through men and knew the thoughts of their hearts. These *depths of Satan* I leave to others to fathom or to dive into as they please, and do not pretend for my own part to know what ideas to affix to such terms, and cannot well guess what conceptions of things these creatures have at these times when they call themselves " all light." But my interpreter informs me that he heard one of them tell a certain Indian the secret thoughts of his heart, which he had never divulged. The case was this: the Indian was bitten with a snake, and in extreme pain. The diviner being applied to for his recovery, told him that at such a time he had promised the next deer he killed should be sacrificed to some great power, but he had broken his promise. And now, said he, that great power has ordered this snake to bite you for your neglect. The Indian confessed it was so, but said he had never told anybody of it. But as Satan, no doubt, excited the Indian to make that promise, it was no wonder he should be able to communicate the matter to the conjurer.

These things serve to fix them down in their idolatry, and to make them believe there is no safety to be expected but by their continuing to offer such sacrifices. And the influence that these Pow-wows have upon them, either through esteem or fear, is no small hindrance to their embracing Christianity.

To remove this difficulty, I have laboured to show the Indians that these diviners have no power to recover the sick, when the God whom Christians serve has determined them for death, and that the supposed great power, who influences these diviners, has himself no power in this case; and that if they seem to recover any by their magic charms, they are only such as the God I preached to them had determined should recover, and who would have recovered without their con-jurations. And when I have apprehended them afraid of embracing Christianity, lest they should be enchanted and poisoned, I have endeavoured to relieve their minds by asking them why their Powwows did not enchant and poison me, seeing they had as much reason to hate me for preaching to them and desiring them to become Christians, as they could have to hate them in case they should actually become such. And that they might have an evidence of the power and good-ness of God engaged for the protection of Christians,

I ventured to bid a challenge to all their Powwows and great powers to do their worst on me first of all, and thus laboured to tread down their influence.

Many things further might be offered upon this head, but this much may suffice for a representation of their aversion to, and prejudice against Christianity, the springs of it, and the difficulties thence arising.

*Secondly,* Another great difficulty I have met with in my attempts to Christianise the Indians, has been to *convey divine truths to their understandings, and to gain their assent to them as such.*

In the *first* place, I laboured under a very great disadvantage for want of an interpreter, who had a good degree of doctrinal as well as experimental knowledge of divine things. In both these respects my present interpreter was very defective when I first employed him, as I noted in the account I before gave of him. And it was sometimes extremely discouraging to me, when I could not make him understand what I designed to communicate; when truths of the last importance appeared *foolishness to him* for want of a spiritual understanding and relish of them; and when he addressed the Indians in a lifeless indifferent manner, without any heart or fervency; especially when he appeared irresolute about making attempts for the conversion of the Indians to Christianity, as he frequently did. For though he had a desire that they should conform to Christian manners, as I elsewhere observed, yet being abundantly acquainted with their strong attachment to their own superstitious notions, and the difficulty of bringing them off, and having no sense of divine power and grace, nor dependence upon an Almighty arm for the accomplishment of this work, he used to be discouraged, and tell me, " It signifies nothing for us to try, they will never turn." So that he was a distressing weight and burden to me. And here I should have sunk scores of times, but that God in a remarkable manner supported me; sometimes by giving me full satisfaction that He Himself had called me to this work, and thence a secret hope that some time or other I might meet with success in it; or if not, that *my judgment should notwithstanding be with the Lord, and my work with my God.* Sometimes by giving me a sense of His almighty power, and that *His hand was not shortened.* Sometimes by affording me a fresh and lively view of some remarkable freedom and assistance I had been repeatedly favoured with in prayer for the ingathering of these heathen some years before, even before I was a missionary, and a refreshing sense of the stability and faithfulness of the divine promises, and that the *prayer of faith* should not fail. Thus I was supported under these trials; and the method God was pleased to take for the removal of the difficulty, respecting my interpreter, I have sufficiently represented elsewhere.

Another thing that rendered it very difficult to convey divine truth to the understanding of the Indians was the *defectiveness* of their language, the want of terms to express and convey ideas of spiritual things. There are no words in the Indian language to answer our English words, "Lord, Saviour, salvation, sinner, justice, condemnation, faith, repentance, justification, adoption, sanctification, grace, glory, heaven," with scores of the like importance.

The only methods I can make use of for surmounting this difficulty are, either to describe the things at large designed by these terms, as, if I was speaking of regeneration, to call it the "heart's being changed" by God's Spirit, or the "heart's being made good." Or else I must introduce the English terms into their language, and fix the precise meaning of them, that they may know what I intend whenever I use them.

But what renders it much more difficult to convey divine truth to the understanding of these Indians is that there seems to be *no foundation in their minds to begin upon*; I mean no truths that may be taken for granted as being already known, while I am attempting to instil others. Divine truths having such a necessary connection with and dependence upon each other, I find it extremely difficult in my first addresses to pagans to begin and discourse of them in their proper order and connection, without having reference to truths not yet known,—without taking for granted such things as need first to be taught and proved. There is no point of Christian doctrine but what they are either wholly ignorant of, or extremely confused in their notions about. Hence it is necessary they should be instructed in every truth, even in those that are the most easy and obvious to the understanding, which a person educated under Gospel-light would be ready to pass over in silence, as not imagining that any rational creature could be ignorant of.

The way I have usually taken in my first addresses to pagans has been to introduce myself by saying that I was come among them with a desire and design of teaching them some things which I presumed they did not know, and which I trusted would be for their comfort and happiness; desiring they would give their attention, and hoping they might meet with satisfaction in my discourse. I have then proceeded to observe that there are two things belonging to every man, which I call the soul and body. These I endeavour to distinguish from each other, by observing that there is something in them that is capable of joy and pleasure, when their bodies are sick and much pained; and on the contrary, that they find something within them that is fearful, sorrowful, ashamed, and consequently very uneasy, when their bodies are in perfect health. I then observe to them that this which rejoices in them (perhaps at the sight of some friend who has been long absent) when their bodies are sick and in pain; this which is sorrowful, frighted, ashamed, and consequently uneasy, when their bodies are perfectly at ease,—this I call the soul. And though it cannot be seen like the other part of the man, the body, yet it is as real as their thoughts and desires, which are likewise things that cannot be seen.

I then further observe that this part of the man which thinks, rejoices, grieves, will live after the body is dead. For the proof of this, I produce the opinion of their fathers, who (as I am told by very aged Indians now living) always supposed there was something of the man that would survive the body. And if for the proof of anything I assert, I can say as St. Paul to the Athenians, *As certain also of your own sages have said*, it is sufficient. Having established this point, I next observe that what I have to say to them respects the *conscious* part of this man, and that with relation to its state after the death of the body; and that I am not come to treat with them about the things that concern the present world.

This method I am obliged to take, because they will otherwise entirely mistake the design of my preaching, and suppose the business I am upon is something that relates to the present world, having never been called together by the white people upon any other occasion, but only to be treated with about the sale of lands or some other secular business. I find it almost impossible to prevent their imagining that I am engaged in the same or such like affairs, and to beat it into them that my concern is to treat with them about their invisible part, and that with relation to its future state. But having thus opened the way by distinguishing between soul and body, and showing the immortality of the former, and that my business is to treat with them in order to their happiness in a future state ; I proceed to discourse of the being and perfections of God, particularly of His eternity, unity, self-sufficiency, infinite wisdom, and almighty power. It is necessary in the first place to teach them that God is from everlasting, and so distinguished from all creatures ; though it is very difficult to communicate anything of that nature to them, they having no terms in their language to signify an eternity *a parte ante*. It is likewise necessary to discourse of the divine unity, in order to confute the notions they seem to have of a plurality of gods. The divine all-sufficiency must also necessarily be mentioned, in order to prevent their imagining that God was unhappy while alone, before the formation of His creatures. Something also respecting the divine wisdom and power seems necessary to be insisted upon, in order to make way for discoursing on God's works.

Having offered some remarks on the divine perfections, I proceed to open the work of *creation* in general, and in particular God's creation of man in a state of uprightness and happiness, placing him in a garden of pleasure; the means and manner of his apostasy from that state, and the loss of that happiness. But before I can relate the history of the Fall, I am obliged to make a large digression, in order to give an account of the origin of the tempter, and the circumstances under which he seduced our first parents. Then I go on to show the ruins of our fallen state, the mental blindness and vicious dispositions our first parents then contracted to themselves and propagated to all their posterity; the numerous calamities brought upon them and theirs by this apostasy from God, and the exposedness of the whole human race to eternal perdition. I then labour to show the necessity of an almighty Saviour to deliver us from this deplorable state, as well as of a divine revelation to instruct and direct us in the will of God.

By such an introductory discourse, the way is prepared for opening the Gospel-scheme of salvation through the great Redeemer, and for treating on those doctrines that immediately relate to our renovation by the divine Spirit, and preparation for a state of everlasting blessedness.

In giving such a relation of things to pagans, it is not a little difficult, as was observed before, to deliver truths in their proper order, without interfering, and without taking for granted things not as yet known; to discourse of them in a familiar manner, suited to the capacities of heathen; to illustrate them by easy and natural similitudes; to obviate or answer the objections they are disposed to make against the several particulars of it, as well as to notice and confute their contrary notions.

What has sometimes been very discouraging in my first discourses to them is that, when I have distinguished between the present and future state, and shown them that it was my business to treat of those things that concern the life to come, they have some of them mocked, looked upon them as things of no importance; have scarcely had a curiosity to hear, and perhaps walked off before I had half done my discourse. In such a case no impressions can be made upon their minds to gain their attention. They are not awed by hearing of the anger of God against sinners, of everlasting punishment as the portion of those who neglect the Gospel, nor allured by hearing of the blessedness of those who embrace and obey it. To gain their attention to my discourse has often been as difficult as to give them a just notion of their design, or to open truths in their proper order.

Another difficulty naturally falling under this head is that *it is next to impossible to bring them to a rational conviction that they are sinners by nature, and that their hearts are corrupt and sinful*, unless one could charge them with some gross acts of immorality, such as the light of nature condemns. If they can be charged with behaviour contrary to the commands of the second table, with manifest abuses of their neighbour, they will generally own such actions to be wrong; but then they seem to think it was only the actions that were sinful, and not their hearts. But if they cannot be charged with such scandalous actions, they have no consciousness of sin and guilt at all, as I had occasion to observe in my Journal of March 24. So that it is very difficult to convince them rationally of that which is readily acknowledged, though, alas! rarely felt in the Christian world, "That we are all sinners."

The method I take to convince them that we are sinners by nature is to lead them to an observation of their little children, how they will appear in a rage, fight and strike their mothers, before they are able to speak or walk, while they are so young that it is plain they are incapable of learning such practices. The light of nature in the Indians condemning such behaviour in children towards their parents, they must own these tempers and actions to be wrong and sinful; and the children having never learned these things, they must have been in their natures, and consequently they must be allowed to be *by nature the children of wrath.* The same I observe to them with respect to the sin of lying, to which their children are much inclined. They tell lies without being taught so to do, from their own natural inclination, as well as against restraints, and after corrections for that vice, which proves them sinners by nature.

To show them that their hearts are all corrupted and sinful, I observe to them that this may be the case, and they not be sensible of it through the blindness of their minds. That it is no evidence they are not sinful, because they do not know and feel it. I then mention all the vices I know the Indians to be guilty of, and so make use of these sinful streams to convince them the fountain is corrupt. And this is the end for which I mention their wicked practices to them, not because I expect to bring them to an effectual reformation merely by inveighing against their immoralities; but hoping they may hereby be convinced of the corruption of their hearts, and awakened to a sense of the depravity and misery of their fallen state. Also to convince them that they are sinners, I sometimes open to them the great command of loving God with all the heart; showing them the reasonableness of loving Him who has made, preserved, and dealt so bountifully with us. I then labour to show them their utter neglect, and that they have been so far from loving God in this manner, that on the contrary, He has not been *in all their thoughts.*

These, and such like, are the means I have made use of in order to remove this difficulty; but if it be asked after all how it was surmounted, I must answer, God Himself was pleased to do it with regard to a number of these Indians, by taking the work into His own hand, and making them feel at heart that they were both sinful and miserable.

And in the *day of God's power,* whatever was spoken to them from God's Word served to convince them they were sinners, even the most melting invitations of the Gospel, and to fill them with solicitude to obtain a deliverance from that deplorable state.

Further, it is extremely difficult to give them any just notion of *the undertaking of Christ in behalf of sinners;* of His obeying and suffering in their room and stead, in order to atone for their sins and procure their salvation; and of their being justified by His righteousness imputed to them. They are in general wholly unacquainted with civil laws and proceedings, and know of no such thing as one person's being substituted as a surety in the room of another, nor have any kind of notion of civil judicatures, of persons being arraigned, tried, judged, condemned, or acquitted. Hence it is very difficult to treat with them upon anything of this nature, or that bears any relation to legal procedures. And though they cannot but have some dealings with the white people, in order to procure clothing and other necessaries of life, yet it is scarcely ever known that any one pays a penny for another, but each one stands for himself. Yet this is a thing that may be supposed, though seldom practised among them, and they may be made to understand that, if a friend of theirs pay a debt for them, it is right that upon that consideration they themselves should be discharged.

This is the only way I can take in order to give them a proper notion of the undertaking and satisfaction of Christ in behalf of sinners. But here naturally arise two questions. *First,* "What need there was of Christ's obeying and suffering for us; why God would not look upon us to be good creatures (to use my common phrase for justification) on account of our own good deeds?" In answer to which I sometimes observe that a child's being ever so orderly and obedient to its parents to-day does by no means satisfy for its contrary behaviour yesterday; and that, if it be loving and obedient at some times only, and at other times cross and disobedient, it never can be looked upon as a good child for its own doings, since it ought to have behaved in an obedient manner always. This simile strikes their minds in an easy and forcible manner, and serves in a measure to illustrate the point. For the light of nature teaches them that their children ought to be obedient to them, and that at all times; and some of them are very severe with them for the contrary behaviour. This I apply in the plainest manner to our behaviour towards God; and so show them that it is impossible for us, since we have sinned against God, to be justified before Him by our own doings, since present and future goodness, although perfect and constant, could never satisfy for past misconduct.

A *second* question is, "If our debt was so great,

and if we all deserved to suffer, how one Person's suffering was sufficient to answer for the whole." Here I have no better way to illustrate the infinite value of Christ's obedience and sufferings, arising from the dignity and excellency of His Person, than to show them the superior value of gold to that of baser metals, and that a small quantity of this will discharge a greater debt than a vast quantity of common copper pence. After all, it is extremely difficult to treat with them upon this great doctrine of justification by imputed righteousness.

I scarcely know how to conclude this head, so many things occurring that might properly be added here; but what has been mentioned may serve for a specimen of the difficulty of conveying divine truths to the understandings of these Indians and of gaining their assent to them as such.

*Thirdly,* Their *inconvenient situations, savage manners, and unhappy method of living,* have been an unspeakable difficulty and discouragement to me in my work.

They generally live in the wilderness, and some that I have visited at great distances from the English settlements, which has obliged me to travel much, and oftentimes over hideous rocks, mountains, and swamps,—frequently to lie out in the open woods, — deprived me of the common comforts of life, and greatly impaired my health.

When I have got among them in the wilderness, I have often met with great difficulty in my attempts to discourse to them. I have spent hours with them in attempting to answer their objections and remove their jealousies, before I could prevail upon them to give me a hearing upon Christianity; have been often obliged to preach in their houses in cold and windy weather, when they have been full of smoke and cinders, as well as unspeakably filthy; which has many times thrown me into violent sick headaches. While I have been preaching, their children have frequently cried to such a degree that I could scarcely be heard, and their pagan mothers would take no manner of care to quiet them. At the same time perhaps some have been laughing and mocking at divine truths; others playing with their dogs, whittling sticks, and the like; and this, in many of them, not from spite and prejudice, but for want of better manners.

A view of these things has been not a little sinking and discouraging to me; it has sometimes prevailed so far as to render me entirely dispirited, and wholly unable to go on with my work; and given me such a melancholy turn of mind that I have many times thought I could never more address an Indian upon religious matters.

The solitary manner in which I have generally been obliged to live, on account of their inconvenient situations, has been not a little pressing. I have spent the greater part of my time, for more than three years past, entirely alone, as to any agreeable society ; and a very considerable part of it I have lived in houses by myself, without having the company of any human creature. Sometimes I have scarcely seen an Englishman for a month or six weeks together. I have also had my spirits so depressed with melancholy views of the temper and conduct of pagans, when I have been for some time confined with them, that I have felt as if banished from all the people of God.

I have likewise been wholly alone in my work, there being no other missionary among the Indians in either of these provinces. And other ministers, knowing neither the peculiar difficulties nor most advantageous methods of performing my work, have not been able to afford me much assistance or support in any respect. Feeling the great dis-advantages of being alone in this work has dis-covered to me the wisdom and goodness of the great Head of the Church, in sending forth His disciples two and two, in order to proclaim the sacred mysteries of His kingdom ; and has made me long for a colleague to be a partner of my cares, hopes, and fears, as well as labours amongst the Indians. This has excited me to use means in order to procure such an assistant, though I have not as yet been so happy as to succeed in that respect.

I have not only met with great difficulty in travelling to, and for some time residing among

the Indians far remote in the wilderness, but also
in living with them in one place and another more
statedly. I have been obliged to remove my residence from place to place; have procured, and
after some poor fashion, furnished three houses for
living among them, in the space of about three
years past. One at Kaunaumeek, about twenty
miles distant from the city of Albany; one at the
Forks of Delaware, in Pennyslvania; and one at
Crossweeksung, in New Jersey. The Indians in
the latter of these provinces, with whom I have
lately spent most of my time, being not long since
removed from the place where they lived the last
winter (the reason of which I mentioned in my
Journal of March 24 and May 4), I have now no
house at all of my own, but am obliged to lodge
with an English family at a considerable distance,
to the great disadvantage of my work among them,
they being like children that continually need
advice and direction, as well as incitement to their
worldly business. The houses I have formerly
lived in are at great distances from each other;
the two nearest of them being more than seventy
miles apart, and neither of them within fifteen
miles of the place where the Indians now live.

The Indians are very poor and indigent, and so
destitute of the comforts of life at some seasons of
the year especially, that it is impossible for a person
who has any pity for them, and concern for the
Christian interest, to live among them without

considerable expense, especially in time of sickness. If anything be bestowed on one, as in some cases it is peculiarly necessary, in order to remove their pagan jealousies and engage their friendship to Christianity; others, be there never so many of them, expect the same treatment. And while they retain their pagan tempers, they discover little gratitude, or even manhood, amidst all the kindnesses they receive. If they make any presents, they expect double satisfaction; and Christianity itself does not at once cure them of these ungrateful and unmanly tempers.

They are in general unspeakably indolent and slothful; have been bred up in idleness; know little about cultivating land, or indeed of engaging vigorously in any other business. So that I am obliged to instruct them in, as well as press them to, the performance of their work, and take the oversight of all their secular concerns. They have little or no ambition or resolution; not one in a thousand of them that has the spirit of a man. It is next to impossible to make them sensible of the duty and importance of being active, diligent, and industrious in the management of their worldly business; and to excite any spirit and promptitude of that nature in them. When I have laboured to the utmost of my ability to show them of what importance it would be to the Christian interest among them, as well as to their worldly comfort, for them to be laborious and prudent in their business, and to furnish themselves with the comforts of life; how this would incline the pagans to come among them, and so put them under the means of salvation; how it would encourage religious persons of the white people to help them, as well as stop the mouths of others that were disposed to cavil against them; how they might by this means pay their just debts, and so prevent trouble from coming upon themselves, and reproach upon their Christian profession : — when I have endeavoured to represent this matter in the most advantageous light I possibly could, they have indeed assented to all I said, but been little moved, and consequently have acted like themselves, or at least too much so. It must at the same time be acknowledged that those who appear to have a sense of divine things are considerably amended in this respect; and it is hopeful that time will make a yet greater alteration upon them for the better.

The concern I have had for the settling of these Indians in New Jersey in a compact form, in order to their being a Christian congregation in a capacity of enjoying the means of grace ; the care of managing their worldly business in order to this end, and to their having a comfortable livelihood, have been more pressing to my mind, and cost me more labour and fatigue for several months past, than all my other work among them.

Their wandering to and fro in order to procure

the necessaries of life is another difficulty that attends my work. This has often deprived me of opportunities to discourse to them; has thrown them in the way of temptation, either among pagans farther remote where they have gone to hunt, who have laughed at them for hearkening to Christianity; or among white people still more horribly wicked, who have often made them drunk; and then got their commodities, such as skins, baskets, brooms, shovels, and the like, with which they designed to have bought corn and other necessaries of life for themselves and families, for it may be nothing but a little strong liquor, and then sent them home empty. So that for the labour perhaps of several weeks, they have got nothing but the satisfaction of being drunk once; and have not only lost labour but, which is infinitely worse, the impressions of divine things that were made upon their minds before. But I forbear enlarging upon this head. The few hints I have given may be sufficient to give thinking persons some apprehensions of the difficulties attending my work, on account of the inconvenient situations and savage manners of the Indians, as well as of their unhappy method of living.

*Fourthly,* The last difficulty I shall mention as having attended my work is *what has proceeded from the attempts that some ill-minded persons have designedly made, to hinder the propagation of the Gospel and a work of divine grace among the Indians.*

The Indians are not only of themselves pre-judiced against Christianity, on the various accounts I have already mentioned, but, as if this was not enough, there are some in all parts of the country where I have preached, who have taken pains industriously to bind them down in pagan dark-ness; neglecting *to enter into the kingdom of God themselves*, and labouring to *hinder others*. After the beginning of the religious concern among the Indians in New Jersey, some endeavoured to pre-judice them against me and the truths I taught them, by the most unmanly and false suggestions of things that had no manner of foundation but in their own brains. Some particulars of this kind I formerly noticed in one of the remarks made upon my Journal concluded in November last. I might have added yet more, and of another nature than those already mentioned, had not modesty forbidden me to mention what was too obscene to be thought of. But through the mercy of God they were never able, by all their abomin-able insinuations and downright lies, to create in the Indians those jealousies they desired to possess them with, and so were never suffered to hinder the work of grace among them.

But when they saw they could not prejudice the Indians against me, nor hinder them from receiving the Gospel, they then noised it through the country that I was undoubtedly a Roman Catholic; that I was gathering together, and training up the Indians in order to serve a popish interest; that I should quickly head them and cut people's throats. The pretended reason for this opinion was that they understood I had a commission from Scotland. They could therefore with great assurance say, "All Scotland is turned to the Pretender, and this is but a popish plot to make a party for him here." And some, I am informed, actually went to the civil authority with complaints against me, only they laboured under this unhappiness that, when they came, they had nothing to complain of, and could give no colour of reason why they attempted any such thing, or desired the civil authority to take cognisance of me, having not a word to allege against my preaching or practice; only they surmised that, because the Indians appeared so very loving and orderly, they had a design of imposing upon people by that means, and so of getting a better advantage to cut their throats! What temper they would have had the Indians to possess, in order to have given no occasion, nor have left any room for such a suspicion, I cannot tell. I presume if they had appeared with the contrary temper it would quickly have been observed of them that they were now grown surly, and in all probability were preparing to "cut people's throats." From a view of these things, I have had occasion to admire the wisdom and goodness of God in providing so full and authentic a commission for the undertaking and carrying on of this work, without which, notwithstanding the charitableness of the design, it had probably met with molestation.

The Indians who have been my hearers in New Jersey have likewise been sued for debt, and threatened with imprisonment more since I came among them, as they inform me, than in seven years before. The reason of this I suppose was, they left frequenting those tippling houses where they used to consume most of what they gained by hunting and other means; and these persons seeing that *the hope of future gain was lost* were resolved to make sure of what they could. And perhaps some of them put the Indians to trouble, purely out of spite at their embracing Christianity. This has been very distressing to me; for I was sensible that, if they did imprison any one who embraced or hearkened to Christianity, the news of it would quickly spread among the pagans hundreds of miles distant, who would immediately conclude that I had involved them in this difficulty, and thence be filled with prejudice against Christianity, and strengthened in their jealousy that the whole of my design was to ensnare and enslave them. I knew that some of the Indians upon Susquehanna had made this objection against hearing me preach,—That they understood a number of Indians in Maryland, some hundred of miles distant, being uncommonly free with the English, were after a-while put in jail and sold. Hence they concluded it was best for them to keep at a distance, and have nothing to do with Christians.

In order to remove this difficulty, I pressed the Indians with all possible speed to pay their debts; exhorting those of them that had skins or money, and were themselves in a good measure free from debt, to help others that were oppressed. Frequently upon such occasions I have paid money out of my own pocket, which I have not as yet received again. These are some of the difficulties I have met with from the conduct of those who, notwithstanding their actions tend so much to hinder the propagation of Christianity, would I suppose be loth to be reputed pagans.

Thus I have endeavoured to answer the demands of the Honourable Society in relation to each of the particulars mentioned in their letter. If what I have written may be in any measure agreeable and satisfactory, and serve to excite in them or any of God's people a spirit of prayer and supplication for the furtherance of a work of grace among the Indians here, and the propagation of it to their distant tribes, I shall have abundant reason to rejoice and bless God in this as well as in other respects.                              D. B.

*June* 20, 1746.

*P.S.*—Since the conclusion of the preceding Journal, which was designed to represent the operations of one year only, from the first time of my preaching to the Indians in New Jersey, I administered the Lord's Supper a second time in my congregation, on the 13th July.

There were more than thirty communicants of the Indians, though divers were absent who should have communicated; so considerably has God enlarged our number since the former solemnity of this kind, described somewhat particularly in my Journal. This appeared to be a season of divine power and grace, not unlike the former; a season of refreshing to God's people in general, and of awakening to some others, although the divine influence manifestly attending the several services of the solemnity seemed not so great and powerful as at the former season.

# SECOND APPENDIX TO THE JOURNAL.

THE deplorable state of the Indians in these parts of America having been represented to the Society in Scotland for Propagating Christian Knowledge, the said Society cheerfully came to the proposal of maintaining two missionaries among these miserable pagans, to endeavour their conversion *from darkness to light, and from the power of Satan unto God*; and sent their commission to some ministers and other gentlemen here to act as their Correspondents, in providing, directing, and inspecting the mission.

As soon as the Correspondents were thus authorised, they immediately looked out for two candidates of the evangelical ministry, whose zeal for the interests of the Redeemer's kingdom, and whose compassion for poor perishing souls, would prompt them to such an exceeding difficult and self-denying undertaking. They first prevailed with Mr. Azariah Horton to relinquish a call to an encouraging parish, and to devote himself to the Indian service. He was directed to Long Island, in August 1741, at the east end of which are two small towns of the Indians, and from the east to the west end of the island lesser companies settled at a few miles' distance from one another, for the length of above a hundred miles.

At his first coming among them he was well received by most, and heartily welcomed by some of them. Those at the east end of the island especially gave diligent and serious attention to his instructions, and were many of them put upon solemn enquiries about *what they should do to be saved.* A general reformation of manners was soon observable among most of these Indians. They were serious and solemn in their attendance upon both public and private instructions. A number of them were under very deep convictions of their miserable perishing state ; and about twenty of them gave lasting evidences of their saving conversion to God. Mr. Horton has baptized thirty-five adults and forty-four children. He took pains to teach them to read; and some of them have made considerable proficiency. But the extensiveness of his charge, and the necessity of his travelling from place to place, make him incapable of giving so constant attendance to their instruction in reading as is needful. In his last letter to the Correspondents, he complains of a great defection from their first reformation and care about their souls, occasioned by strong drink being brought among them, and their being thereby allured to a relapse into their darling vice of drunkenness: a vice to which the Indians are everywhere so greatly addicted, and so vehemently disposed, that nothing but the power of divine grace can restrain that impetuous lust, when they have opportunity to gratify it.

He likewise complains that some of them are grown more careless and remiss in the duties of religious worship than they were when first acquainted with the great things of their eternal peace. But as a number retain their first impressions, and as they generally attend with reverence upon his ministry, he goes on with encouraging hopes of the presence and blessing of God with him in his difficult undertaking.

This is a general view of the state of the mission upon Long Island, collected from several of Mr.

Horton's letters; which is all that could now be offered, not having as yet a particular account from Mr. Horton himself.

It was some time after Mr. Horton was employed in the Indian service, before the Correspondents could obtain another qualified candidate for this self-denying mission. At length they prevailed with Mr. David Brainerd to refuse several invitations to places where he had a promising prospect of a comfortable settlement among the English, to encounter the fatigues and perils that must attend his carrying the Gospel of Christ to these poor miserable savages. A general representation of his conduct and success in that undertaking is contained in a letter we lately received from himself, which is as follows :—

To THE REV. EBENEZER PEMBERTON.

REV. SIR,—Since you are pleased to require of me some brief and general account of my conduct in the affair of my mission amongst the Indians, the pains and endeavours I have used to propagate Christian knowledge among them, the difficulties I have met with in pursuance of that great work, and the hopeful and encouraging appearances I have observed in any of them ; I shall now endeavour to answer your demands, by giving a brief but faithful account of the most material things relating to that important affair, with which I have been and am still concerned. And this I shall do with more freedom and cheerfulness, both because I apprehend it will be a likely means to give pious persons, who are concerned for the kingdom of Christ, some just apprehension of the difficulties that attend the propagation of it amongst the poor pagans; and, it is hoped, will engage their more frequent and fervent prayers to God that those may be succeeded who are employed in this arduous work; and also because I persuade myself that the tidings of the Gospel's spreading among the poor heathen will be, to those who are waiting for the accomplishment of the *glorious things spoken of the city of our God*, as *good news from a far country*; and that *these* will be so far from *despising the day of small things*, that, on the contrary, the least dawn of encouragement and hope in this important affair will rather inspire their pious breasts with warmer desires, that *the kingdoms of this world may speedily become the kingdom of our Lord and of His Christ.*

I shall therefore immediately proceed to the business before me, and briefly touch upon the most important matters concerning my mission, from the beginning to this present time.

On March 15, 1743, I waited on the Correspondents for the Indian mission at New York; and the week following attended their meeting at Woodbridge in New Jersey, and was speedily dismissed by them with orders to attempt the instruction of a number of Indians in a place some miles distant from the city of Albany. On the first of April following I arrived among the Indians at a place called by them Kaunaumeek, in the county of Albany, about twenty miles distant from the city eastward.

The place was sufficiently lonesome and unpleasant, being encompassed with mountains and woods, twenty miles distant from any English inhabitants, six or seven from any Dutch, and more than two from a family that came some time since from the Highlands of Scotland, and had then lived about two years in this wilderness. In this family I lodged about the space of three months, the master of it being the only person with whom I could readily converse in those parts, except my interpreter, others understanding very little English.

After I had spent about three months in this situation, I found my distance from the Indians a very great disadvantage to my work amongst them, and very burdensome to myself. I was obliged to travel forward and backward almost daily on foot, having no pasture in which I could keep a horse for that purpose. After all my pains, I could not be with the Indians in the evening and morning, which were usually the best hours to find them at home, and when they could best attend my instructions. I therefore resolved to remove and live with or near the Indians, that I might watch all opportunities, when they were generally at home, and take the advantage of such seasons for their instruction. I accordingly removed soon after; and for a time, lived with them in one of their wigwams. I then built a small house, where I spent the remainder of that year entirely alone; my interpreter, who was an Indian, choosing rather to live in a wigwam among his own countrymen.

This way of living was attended with many difficulties. I found myself in a place where I could get none of the necessaries and common comforts of life; no, not so much as a morsel of bread, but what I brought from places fifteen and twenty miles distant; and was often obliged for some time together to content myself without, for want of an opportunity to procure the things I needed. But though the difficulties of this solitary way of living are not the least or most inconsiderable (and doubtless are in fact many more and greater to those who experience them than they can readily appear to those who only view them at a distance); yet I can truly say that the burden I felt respecting my great work among the poor Indians, the fear and concern lest they should be prejudiced against Christianity, and their minds embittered against me and my labours among them, by means of the insinuations of some who, though they are called Christians, seem to have no concern for Christ's kingdom, but had rather that the Indians should remain heathen, that they may with the more ease cheat and so enrich themselves by them;—I say, the fear and concern I felt in these respects were much more pressing to me than all the difficulties that attended the circumstances of my living.

As to the state or temper of mind in which I found these Indians, at my first coming among them, I may justly say, it was much more desirable and encouraging than what appears among those who are altogether uncultivated. Their heathenish jealousies and suspicion, and their prejudices against Christianity, were in a great measure removed by the long-continued labours of the Rev. Mr. Sargeant among a number of the same tribe, in a place little more than twenty miles distant. The Indians were in some good degree prepared to entertain the truths of Christianity; instead of objecting against them, and appearing almost entirely untractable, as is common with them at first, and as perhaps these appeared a few years ago. Some of them at least appeared very well-disposed toward religion, and were much pleased with my coming among them.

In order to *turn them from darkness to light*, I studied what was most plain and easy and best suited to their capacities. I endeavoured to set before them from time to time, as they were able to receive them, the most important and necessary truths of Christianity; such as immediately concerned their conversion to God, and such as I judged had the greatest tendency to effect that glorious change in them. Especially I made it the scope and drift of all my labours, to lead them into a thorough acquaintance with these two things. *First,* The sinfulness and misery of their state by nature; the evil of their hearts, the heavy guilt they were under, and their exposedness to everlasting punishment; also their utter inability to save themselves, either from their sins or from their miseries, which are the just punishment of them; their unworthiness of any mercy at the hand of God, on account of anything they themselves could do to procure His favour, and consequently their extreme need of Christ to save them.

*Secondly,* I frequently endeavoured to open to them the fulness, all-sufficiency, and freeness of that redemption, which the Son of God has wrought out by His obedience and sufferings for perishing sinners; how this provision was suited to all their wants; and how He called and invited them to accept of everlasting life freely, notwithstanding all their sinfulness, inability, and unworthiness.

After I had been with the Indians several months, I composed some Forms of Prayer, adapted to their circumstances and capacities; which, with the help of my interpreter, I translated into the Indian language; and soon learned to pronounce their words, so as to pray with them in their own tongue. I also translated several Psalms into their language, and soon after we were able to sing in the worship of God. When the people had gained some acquaintance with the truths of Christianity, so that they were capable of receiving and understanding many others, which at first could not be taught them, by reason of their ignorance of those that were necessarily to be previously known, and upon which others depended; I then gave them an historical account of God's dealings with His ancient professing people the Jews; some of the rites and ceremonies they were obliged to observe, and what these were designed to represent; also some of the surprising miracles God wrought for their salvation, while they trusted in Him, and the sore punishments He sometimes brought upon them, when they forsook and sinned against Him. Afterwards I proceeded to give them a relation of the birth, life, miracles, sufferings, death, and resurrection of Christ; as well as His ascension, and the wonderful effusion of the Holy Spirit consequent upon it.

Having thus endeavoured to prepare the way by such a general account of things, I next proceeded to read and expound to them the Gospel of St. Matthew, at least the substance of it, which afforded them a more distinct and particular view of what they had before learned. These expositions I attended almost every evening, when there was any considerable number of them at home; except when I was obliged to be absent myself, in order to learn the Indian language with the Rev. Mr. Sargeant. There was likewise an English school constantly kept by my interpreter among the Indians; which I used frequently to visit, in order to give the children and young people some instructions and exhortations suited to their age.

The degree of knowledge to which some of them attained was considerable. Many of the truths of Christianity seemed fixed in their minds, especially in some instances ; so that they would speak to me of them, and ask such questions about them, as were 'necessary to render them more plain and clear to their understandings. Some of the children also and young people who attended the school made considerable proficiency in their learning ; so that, had they understood the English language well, they would have been able to read somewhat readily in a psalter.

But that which was most of all desirable, and gave me the greatest encouragement amidst many difficulties and disconsolate hours, was that the truths of God's Word seemed at times to be attended with some power upon the hearts and consciences of the Indians. This appeared evident in a few instances, in which some were awakened to a sense of their miserable state by nature, and appeared solicitous for deliverance from it. Several came of their own accord to discourse with me about their souls; and others with tears enquired *what they should do to be saved* ; and whether the God that Christians served would be merciful to those that had been frequently drunk. And though I cannot say I have satisfactory evidence of their being *renewed in the spirit of their mind,* and savingly converted to God; yet the Spirit of God did in such a manner attend the means of grace, and so operate upon their minds as to afford encouragement to hope that God designed good to them, and that He was preparing His way into their souls.

There likewise appeared a reformation in the lives and manners of the Indians. Their idolatrous sacrifices, of which there was but one or two, that I know of, after my coming among them, were wholly laid aside, as well as their heathenish custom of dancing and hallooing. And I could not but hope that they were reformed in some measure from the sin of drunkenness. They likewise manifested a regard to the Lord's day; and not only behaved soberly themselves, but took care also to keep their children in order. Yet after all I must confess that, as there were many hopeful appearances among them, so there were some things more discouraging. And while I rejoiced to observe any serious concern among them about their souls, still I was not without continual fear and concern, lest such encouraging appearances might prove *like a morning-cloud that passeth away.*

When I had spent near a year with the Indians, I informed them that I expected to leave them in the spring then approaching, and to be sent to another tribe of Indians at a great distance. On hearing this they appeared very sorrowful, and some of them endeavoured to persuade me to continue with them; urging that they had now heard so much about their souls' concerns, that they could never more be willing to live as they had done without a minister and further instructions in the way to heaven. I told them they ought to be willing that others also should hear the Gospel, seeing they needed it as much as themselves. Yet further to dissuade me from going, they added that those Indians, to whom I had thoughts of going, as they had heard, were not willing to become Christians as they were, and therefore urged me to tarry with them. I then told them that they might receive further instruction without me; but the Indians to whom I expected to be sent could not, there being no minister near to teach them. I then advised them, in case I should leave them and be sent elsewhere, to remove to Stockbridge, where they might be supplied with land and conveniences of living, and be under the ministry of the Rev. Mr. Sargeant. They seemed disposed to comply with this advice.

On April 6, 1744, I was directed by the Correspondents for the Indian Mission to take leave of the people, with whom I had then spent a full year, and to go as soon as convenient to a tribe of Indians on Delaware River, in Pennsylvania. On the 29th I took my leave of the people, who were mostly removed to Stockbridge, under the care of the Rev. Mr. Sargeant. I then set out on my journey toward Delaware; and on May 10th met with a number of Indians in a place called Minnissinks, about a hundred and forty miles from Kaunaumeek, the place where I spent the last year, and directly in my way to Delaware River. With these Indians I spent some time, and first addressed their king in a friendly manner. After some discourse, and attempts to contract a friendship with him, I told him I had a desire, for his benefit and happiness, to instruct them in Christianity. He laughed at it, turned his back upon me, and went away. I then addressed another principal man in the same manner, who said he was willing to hear me. After some time I followed the king into his house, and renewed my discourse to him; but he declined talking, and left the affair to another, who appeared to be a rational man. He began and talked very warmly near a quarter of an hour. He enquired why I desired the Indians to become Christians, seeing the Christians were so much worse than the Indians. The Christians, he said, would lie, steal, and drink, worse than the Indians. It was they who first taught the Indians to be drunk; and they stole from one another to that degree, that their rulers were obliged to hang them for it, and yet it was not sufficient to deter others from the like practice. But the Indians, he added, were none of them ever hanged for stealing, and yet they did not steal half so much; and he supposed that, if the Indians should become Christians, they would then be as bad as these. They would live as their fathers lived, and go where their fathers were when they died. I then freely owned, lamented, and joined with him in condemning the ill conduct of some who are called Christians; told him these were not Christians in heart; that I hated such wicked practices, and did not desire the Indians to become such as these. When he appeared calmer, I asked him if he was willing that I should come and see them again: he replied he should be willing to see me again as a friend, if I would not desire them to become Christians. I then bid them farewell, and prosecuted my journey toward Delaware. On May 13th I arrived at a place called by the Indians Sakhauwotung, within the Forks of Delaware, in Pennsylvania.

Here also, when I came to the Indians, I saluted their king and others, in a manner I thought most engaging; and soon after informed the king of my desire to instruct them in the Christian religion. After he had consulted a few minutes with two or three old men, he told me he was willing to hear. I then preached to the few that were present; they appeared very attentive and well-disposed. The king in particular seemed both to wonder and at the same time to be well pleased with what I taught them, respecting the divine Being. Since that time he has ever shown himself friendly, giving me free liberty to preach in his house, whenever I think fit. Here therefore I have spent the greater part of the summer past, preaching usually in the king's house.

The number of Indians in this place is but small; most of those that formerly dwelt here are dispersed, and removed to places farther back in the country. There are not more than ten houses that continue to be inhabited; and some of these are several miles distant from others, which makes it difficult for the Indians to meet together so frequently as could be wished.

When I first began to preach here, the number of hearers was very small; often not exceeding twenty or twenty-five; but towards the latter part of the summer their number increased, so that I have frequently had forty persons or more at once. The effects of God's Word upon some of the Indians in this place are somewhat encouraging. Several of them are brought to renounce idolatry, and to decline partaking of those feasts which they used to offer in sacrifice to certain unknown powers. Some few among them have for a considerable time manifested a serious concern about their eternal welfare, and still continue to *enquire the way to Zion* with such diligence, affection, and becoming solicitude, as gives me reason to hope that God, who (I trust) *has begun this work* in them, will carry it on until it shall issue in their conversion to Himself. These not only detest their old idolatrous notions, but strive also to bring their friends off from them; and, as they are seeking salvation for their own souls, so they seem desirous that others might be excited to do the same.

In July last I heard of a number of Indians residing at a place called Kauksesauchung, more than thirty miles westward from the place where I usually preach. I visited them, found about thirty persons, and proposed to preach to them. They readily complied, and I preached to them only twice, they being just then removing from this place, where they only lived for the present, to Susquehanna River, where they belonged.

While I was preaching they appeared sober and attentive, and were somewhat surprised, having never before heard of these things. Two or three, who suspected that I had some ill design upon them, urged that the white people had abused them, and taken their lands from them; and therefore they had no reason to think that they were now concerned for their happiness; but, on the contrary, that they designed to make them slaves, or get them on board their vessels, and make them fight with the people over the water, as they expressed it, meaning the French and Spaniards. However, most of them appeared very friendly, and told me they were then going directly home to Susquehanna. They desired I would make them a visit there, and manifested a considerable desire of further instruction. This invitation gave me some encouragement in my great work, and made me hope that God designed to *open an effectual door* for spreading the Gospel among the poor heathen farther westward.

In the beginning of October last, with the advice and direction of the Correspondents for the Indian Mission, I undertook a journey to Susquehanna. After three days' tedious travel, two of them through a wilderness, almost impassable by reason of mountains and rocks, and two nights lodging in the open wilderness, I came to an Indian settlement on the side of Susquehanna River, called Opeholhaupung. Here were twelve Indian houses, and about seventy souls, old and young, belonging to them. Here also, soon after my arrival, I visited the king; addressing him with expressions of kindness, and informing him of my desire to teach them the knowledge of Christianity. He hesitated not long before he told me that he was willing to hear. I then preached; and continued there several days, preaching every day, as long as the Indians were at home. And they, in order to hear me, deferred the design of their general hunting, which they were just then entering upon, for the space of three or four days.

The men, I think, universally, except one, attended my preaching. The women, supposing the affair to be of a public nature, belonging only to the men, and not what every individual person should concern himself with, could not readily be

254 SECOND APPENDIX TO JOURNAL

persuaded to come and hear; but, after much pains used with them for that purpose, some few ventured to come and stand at a distance.

When I had preached to the Indians several times, some of them very frankly proposed what they had to object against Christianity; and so gave me a fair opportunity for using my best endeavours to remove from their minds those scruples and jealousies they laboured under. When I had endeavoured to answer their objections, some appeared much satisfied. I then asked the king whether he was willing I should visit and preach to them again, if I should live to the next spring. He replied he should be heartily willing for his own part, and wished the young people would learn. I then put the same question to the rest; some answered they should be very glad, and none manifested any dislike to it.

Other things in their behaviour appeared comfortable and encouraging. Upon the whole I could not but rejoice that I had taken the journey among them, though it was attended with many difficulties and hardships. The instructions I gave them tended in some measure to remove their heathenish jealousies and prejudices against Christianity; and I could not but hope that the God of all grace was preparing their minds to receive *the truth as it is in Jesus.* If this may be the happy consequence, I shall not only rejoice in my past labours and fatigues; but shall I trust also be *willing to spend and be spent,* if I may thereby be instrumental to *turn them from darkness to light, and from the power of Satan to God.*

Thus, Sir, I have given you a faithful account of what has been most considerable respecting my mission among the Indians; in which I have studied all convenient brevity. I shall only now take leave to add a word or two respecting the *difficulties* that attend the Christianising of these poor pagans.

In the first place, their minds are filled with prejudices against Christianity, on account of the vicious lives and unchristian behaviour of some that are called Christians. These not only set before them the worst examples, but some of them take pains, expressly in words, to dissuade them from becoming Christians; foreseeing that, if these should be converted to God, the hope of their unlawful gain would thereby be lost.

Again, these poor heathens are extremely attached to the customs, traditions, and fabulous notions of their fathers. And this one seems to be the foundation of all their other notions, that "it was not the same God made them, who made the white people," but another, who commanded them to live by hunting, and not conform to the customs of the white people. Hence when they are desired to become Christians, they frequently reply that "they will live as their fathers lived, and go to their fathers when they die." If the miracles

of Christ and His apostles be mentioned, to prove
the truth of Christianity, they also mention miracles
which their fathers told them were anciently
wrought among the Indians, and which Satan
makes them believe were so. They are much
attached to idolatry; frequently making feasts,
which they eat in honour of some unknown beings,
who they suppose speak to them in dreams, promising them success in hunting and other affairs,
in case they will sacrifice to them. They also
offer sacrifices to the spirits of the dead; who, they
suppose, stand in need of favours from the living,
and yet are in such a state as they can well reward
all the offices of kindness that are shown them.
And they impute all their calamities to the neglect
of these sacrifices.

Furthermore, they are much awed by those
among themselves, who are called Powwows, who
are supposed to have a power of enchanting, or
poisoning them to death, or at least in a very distressing manner; and they apprehend it would be
their sad fate to be thus enchanted, in case they
should become Christians.

Lastly, their manner of living is likewise a great
disadvantage to the design of their being Christianised. They are almost continually roving from
place to place; and it is but rare that an opportunity can be had with some of them for their
instruction. There is scarce any time of the year
in which the men can be found generally at home,

except about six weeks before and in the season of planting their corn, and about two months in the latter part of summer, from the time they begin to roast their corn until it is fit to gather in.

As to the hardships that necessarily attend a mission among them, the fatigues of frequent journeying in the wilderness, the unpleasantness of a mean and hard way of living, and the great difficulty of addressing a people of a strange language, these I shall at present pass over in silence; designing what I have already said of difficulties attending this work, not for the discouragement of any, but rather for the incitement of all who *love the appearing and kingdom of Christ,* to frequent the Throne of Grace with earnest supplications that the heathen, who were anciently promised to Christ *for His inheritance,* may now actually and speedily be brought into His kingdom of grace, and made heirs of immortal glory.—I am, Sir, your most obedient servant,

DAVID BRAINERD.

THE FORKS OF DELAWARE, IN
PENNSYLVANIA; *Nov.* 5, 1744.

*P.S.*—It should have been observed in the preceding account that, although the number of Indians in the place I visited on Susquehanna River, in October last, is but small, yet their numbers in the adjacent places are very considerable; who it is hoped might be brought to embrace Christianity by the example of others. But being at present somewhat more savage and unacquainted with the English than these I visited, I thought it not best to make my first attempts among them; hoping I might hereafter be better introduced to them by means of these. Several of the neighbouring settlements are much larger than this; so that there are, probably, several hundreds of the Indians not many miles distant.                               D. B.

# THE REMAINS OF DAVID BRAINERD.

## I.—A Dialogue between the Various Powers and Affections of the Pious Mind.

1. The *Understanding* introduced, (1) As discovering its own excellency, and capacity of enjoying the most sublime pleasure and happiness. (2) As observing its desire equal to its capacity, and incapable of being satisfied with anything that will not fill it in the utmost extent of its exercise. (3) As finding itself dependent, not self-sufficient; and consequently unable to spin happiness (as the spider spins its web) out of its own bowels. This self-sufficiency observed to be the property and prerogative of God alone, and not belonging to any created being. (4) As in vain seeking sublime pleasure, satisfaction, and happiness adequate to its nature, amongst created beings. The search and knowledge of the truth in the natural world allowed indeed to be refreshing to the mind, but still failing to afford complete happiness. (5) As discovering the excellency and glory of God, that He is the

fountain of goodness and well-spring of happiness, and every way fit to answer the enlarged desires and cravings of our immortal souls.

2. The *Will* introduced, as necessarily yet freely choosing this God for its supreme happiness and only portion, fully complying with the dictates of the understanding, acquiescing in God as the best good, His will as the best rule for intelligent creatures, and rejoicing that He is in every respect just what He is; and withal choosing and delighting to be a dependent creature, always subject to this God, not aspiring after self-sufficiency and supremacy, but acquiescing in the contrary.

3. Ardent *Love* or *Desire* introduced, as passionately longing to please and glorify the divine Being, to be in every respect conformed to Him, and in that way to enjoy Him. This love or desire represented as most genuine; not induced by mean and mercenary views; not primarily springing from selfish hopes of salvation, whereby the divine glories would be sacrificed to the idol self; not arising from a slavish fear of divine anger in case of neglect, nor yet from hopes of feeling the sweetness of that tender and pleasant passion of love in one's own breast, but from a just esteem of the beauteous object beloved. This Love further represented as attended with vehement longings after the enjoyment of its object, but unable to find by what means.

4. The *Understanding* again introduced, as inform-

ing, (1) How God might have been enjoyed, yea, how He must necessarily have been enjoyed, had not man sinned against Him; that as there was knowledge, likeness, and love, so there must needs be enjoyment, while there was no impediment. (2) How He may be enjoyed in some measure now, namely, by the same knowledge, begetting likeness and love, which will be answered with returns of love and the smiles of God's countenance, which are better than life. (3) How God may be perfectly enjoyed, namely, by the soul's perfect freedom from sin. This perfect freedom never obtained till death; and then not by any unaccountable means or in any unheard of manner; but the same by which it has obtained some likeness to and fruition of God in this world, namely, a clear manifestation of Him.

5. *Holy Desire* appears, and enquires why the soul may not be perfectly holy; and so perfect in the enjoyment of God here; and expresses most insatiable thirstings after such a temper, and such fruition, and most consummate blessedness.

6. *Understanding* again appears, and informs that God designs that those whom He sanctifies in part here, and intends for immortal glory, shall tarry a while in this present evil world, that their own experience of temptations may teach them how great the deliverance is which God has wrought for them, that they may be swallowed up in thankfulness and admiration to eternity; as also that they

may be instrumental of doing good to their fellow-men. Now if they were perfectly holy, a world of sin would not be a fit habitation for them; and further, such manifestations of God as are necessary completely to sanctify the soul would be insupport-able to the body, so that we cannot see God and live.

7. *Holy Impatience* is next introduced, complain-ing of the sins and sorrows of life, and almost repining at the distance of a state of perfection, uneasy to see and feel the hours hang so dull and heavy, and almost concluding that the temptations, hard-ships, disappointments, imperfections, and tedious employments of life will never come to a happy period.

8. *Tender Conscience* comes in, and meekly re-proves the complaints of Impatience; urging how careful and watchful we ought to be, lest we should offend the divine Being with complaints; alleging also the fitness of our waiting patiently upon God for all we want, and that in a way of doing and suffering; and at the same time mentioning the barrenness of the soul, how much precious time is misimproved, and how little it has enjoyed of God, compared with what it might have done; as also suggesting how frequently impatient complaints spring from nothing better than self-love, want of resignation, and a greater reverence of the divine Being.

9. *Judgment* or *Sound Mind* next appears, and

duly weighs the complaints of Impatience, and the gentle admonitions of Tender Conscience, and impartially determines between them.  On the one hand it concludes that we may always be impatient with sin ; and supposes that we may also with such sorrow, pain, and discouragement, as hinder our pursuit of holiness, though they arise from the weakness of nature.  It allows us to be impatient of the distance at which we stand from a state of perfection and blessedness.  It further indulges impatience at the delay of time, when we desire the period of it for no other end than that we may with angels be employed in the most lively spiritual acts of devotion, and in giving all possible glory to Him that lives for ever.  Temptations and sinful imperfections, it thinks we may justly be uneasy with ; and disappointments, at least those that relate to our hopes of communion with God and growing conformity to Him.  And as to the tedious employments and hardships of life, it supposes some longing for the end of them not inconsistent with a spirit of faithfulness, and a cheerful disposition to perform the one and endure the other ; it supposes that a faithful servant, who fully designs to do all he possibly can, may still justly long for the evening ; and that no rational man would blame his kind and tender spouse, if he perceived her longing to be with him, while yet faithfulness and duty to him might still induce her to yield, for the present, to remain at a painful distance from him.

On the other hand, it approves of the caution, care, and watchfulness of Tender Conscience, lest the divine Being should be offended with impatient complaints; it acknowledges the fitness of our *waiting upon God,* in a way of patient doing and suffering; but supposes this very consistent with ardent desires to *depart and to be with Christ.* It owns it fit that we should always remember our own barrenness, and thinks also that we should be impatient of it, and consequently long for a state of freedom from it; and this, not so much that we may feel the happiness of it, but that God may have the glory. It grants that impatient complaints often spring from self-love, and want of resignation and humility. Such as these it disapproves; and determines we should be impatient only of absence from God, and distance from that state and temper wherein we may most glorify Him.

10. *Godly Sorrow* introduced, as making her sad moan, not so much that she is kept from the free possession and full enjoyment of happiness, but that God must be dishonoured; the soul being still in a world of sin, and itself imperfect. She here, with grief, counts over past faults, present temptations, and fears for the future.

11. *Hope* or *Holy Confidence* appears, and seems persuaded that *nothing shall ever separate the soul from the love of God in Christ Jesus.* It expects divine assistance and grace sufficient for all the doing and suffering work of time, and that death

will ere long put a happy period to all sin and
sorrow ; and so takes occasion to rejoice.

12. *Godly Fear* or *Holy Jealousy* here steps in,
and suggests some timorous apprehensions of the
danger of deception ; mentions the deceitfulness of
the heart, the great influence of irregular self-love
in a fallen creature ; enquires whether itself is not
likely to have fallen in with delusion, since the
mind is so dark, and so little of God appears to the
soul ; and queries whether all its hopes of persevering grace may not be presumption, and whether its
confident expectations of meeting death as a friend
may not issue in disappointment.

13. Hereupon *Reflection* appears, and reminds
the person of his past experiences ; as to the
preparatory work of conviction and humiliation ;
the view he then had of the impossibility of
salvation from himself or any created arm ; the
manifestation he has likewise had of the glory of
God in Jesus Christ ; how he then admired that
glory, and chose that God for his only portion,
because of the excellency and amiableness he discovered in Him ; not from slavish fear of being
damned, if he did not, nor from base and mercenary
hopes of saving himself ; but from a just esteem of
that beauteous and glorious Object ; as also how he
had from time to time rejoiced and acquiesced in
God, for what He is in Himself ; being delighted
that He is infinite in holiness, justice, power,
sovereignty, as well as in mercy, goodness, and

love; how he has likewise, scores of times, felt his
soul mourn for sin, for this very reason, because it
is contrary and grievous to God; yea, how he has
mourned over one vain and impertinent thought,
when he has been so far from fear of the divine
vindictive wrath for it, that on the contrary he has
enjoyed the highest assurance of the divine everlasting love; how he has, from time to time,
delighted in the commands of God, for their own
purity and perfection, and longed exceedingly to
be conformed to them, and even to be *holy as God
is holy*; and counted it present heaven to be of a
heavenly temper; how he has frequently rejoiced
to think of being for ever subject to and dependent
on God; accounting it infinitely greater happiness
to glorify God in a state of subjection to and
dependence on Him, than to be a god himself;
and how heaven itself would be no heaven to him,
if he could not there be everything that God would
have him be.

14. Upon this, *Spiritual Sensation*, being awaked,
comes in, and declares that she now feels and
*tastes that the Lord is gracious*; that He is the only
supreme good, the only soul-satisfying happiness;
that He is a complete, self-sufficient, and almighty
portion. She whispers, *Whom have I in heaven* but
this God, this dear and blessed portion, *and there
is none upon earth I desire besides Him*. O, it is
heaven to please Him, and to be just what He
would have me be! O that my soul were holy as

God is holy; pure as Christ is pure; and perfect as my *Father in heaven is perfect*! These are the sweetest commands in God's book, comprising all others; and shall I break them? must I break them? am I under a fatal necessity of it, as long as I live in this world? O my soul! Woe, woe, is me, that I am a sinner; because I now necessarily grieve and offend this blessed God, who is infinite in goodness and grace. O, methinks, should He punish me for my sins, it would not wound my heart so deep to offend Him; but, though I sin continually, He continually repeats His kindness towards me! I could bear any suffering; but how can I bear to grieve and dishonour this blessed God? How shall I give ten thousand times more honour to Him? What shall I do to glorify and worship this Best of beings? O that I could consecrate myself, soul and body, to His service for ever! O that I could give up myself to Him, so as never more to attempt to be my own, or to have any will or affections that are not perfectly conformed to His! But alas, I cannot, I feel I cannot, be thus entirely devoted to God: I cannot live and sin not. O ye angels, do ye glorify Him incessantly; if possible, exert yourselves still more in lively and ardent devotion; if possible, prostrate yourselves still lower before the throne of the blessed King of heaven. I long to bear a part with you, and, if it were possible, to help you. Yet when we have done, we shall not be able to

offer the ten thousandth part of the homage He is
worthy of. While Spiritual Sensation whispered
these things, Fear and Jealousy were greatly over-
come; and the soul replied, *Now I know and am
assured*, and again it welcomed death as a friend,
saying, *O death, where is thy sting?*

15. Finally, *Holy Resolution* concludes the discourse, fixedly determining to *follow hard after God*,
and continually to pursue a life of conformity to
Him. And the better to pursue this, enjoining it
on the soul always to remember that God is the
only source of happiness, that His will is the only
rule of rectitude to an intelligent creature, that
earth has nothing in it desirable for itself, or any
further than God is seen in it; and that the
knowledge of God in Christ, begetting and maintaining love, and mortifying sensual and fleshly
appetites, is the way to be holy on earth, and so
to be attempered to the complete holiness of the
heavenly world.


II.—Desponding Thoughts of a Soul under
Convictions of Sin.


1. I believe my case is singular, that none ever
had so many strange and different thoughts and
feelings as I.

2. I have been concerned much longer than
many others that I have known or read of, who
have been savingly converted, and yet I am left.

3. I have withstood the power of convictions a long time; and therefore I fear I shall be finally left of God.

4. I never shall be converted, without stronger convictions and greater terrors of conscience.

5. I do not aim at the glory of God in anything I do, and therefore I cannot hope for mercy.

6. I do not see the evil nature of sin, nor the sin of my nature; and therefore I am discouraged.

7. The more I strive, the more blind and hard my heart is, and the worse I grow continually.

8. I fear that God never showed mercy to one so vile as I.

9. I fear I am not elected, and therefore must perish.

10. I fear the day of grace is past with me.

11. I fear I have committed the unpardonable sin.

12. I am an old sinner; and if God had designed mercy for me, He would have called me home to Himself before now.

### III.—Signs of Godliness, or the Distinguishing Marks of a True Christian.

1. He has a true knowledge of the glory and excellency of God, that He is most worthy to be loved and praised for His own divine perfections.

2. God is his portion. And God's glory his great concern.

3. Holiness is his delight; nothing he so much longs for as to be holy, as God is holy.

4. Sin is his greatest enemy. This he hates for its own nature, for what it is in itself, being contrary to a holy God. Consequently he hates all sin.

5. The laws of God also are his delight. These he observes, not out of constraint, from a servile fear of hell; but they are his choice. The strict observance of them is not his bondage, but his greatest liberty.


IV.—LETTERS.

TO HIS BROTHER JOHN, AT YALE COLLEGE.

KAUNAUMEEK, *April* 30, 1743.

DEAR BROTHER,—I should tell you, " I long to see you," but that my own experience has taught me there is no happiness and plenary satisfaction to be enjoyed in earthly friends, though ever so near and dear, or in any other enjoyment that is not God Himself. Therefore if the God of all grace would be pleased to afford us each His presence and grace, that we may perform the work and endure the trials He calls us to, in a most distressing tiresome wilderness, till we arrive at our journey's end; the distance at which we are held from each other at the present is a matter of no great moment or importance to either of us. But alas, the presence of God is what I want.

I live in the most lonely melancholy desert,

about eighteen miles from Albany; for it was not thought best that I should go to Delaware River, as I believe I hinted to you in a letter from New York. I board with a poor Scotsman; his wife can talk scarcely any English. My diet consists mostly of hasty-pudding, boiled corn, and bread baked in ashes, and sometimes a little meat and butter. My lodging is a little heap of straw, laid upon some boards, a little way from the ground; for it is a log-room, without any floor, that I lodge in. My work is exceeding hard and difficult; I travel on foot a mile and half in the worst of roads almost daily, and back again; for I live so far from my Indians. I have not seen an English person this month. These and many other uncomfortable circumstances attend me; and yet my spiritual conflicts and distresses so far exceed all these that I scarce think of them, but feel as if I were entertained in the most sumptuous manner. The Lord grant that I may learn to *endure hardness, as a good soldier of Jesus Christ!*

As to my success here, I cannot say much as yet. The Indians seem generally kind and well disposed towards me, and are mostly very attentive to my instructions, and seem willing to be taught. Two or three, I hope, are under some convictions; but there seems to be little of the special workings of the divine Spirit among them yet; which gives me many a heart-sinking hour. Sometimes, I hope, God has abundant blessings in store for them and me; at other times I am so overwhelmed with distress that I cannot see how His dealings with me are consistent with covenant love and faithfulness. And I say, *Surely His tender mercies are clean gone for ever.* But I see, I needed all this chastisement already. *It is good for me* that I have endured these trials, and have hitherto little or no apparent success. Do not be discouraged on my account. I was under great distress at Mr. Pomroy's, when I saw you last; but God has been with me of a truth since that, at Long Island and elsewhere.

Let us always remember that we must *through much tribulation* enter into God's eternal kingdom of rest and peace. The righteous are *scarcely* saved; it is an infinite wonder that we have well-grounded hopes of being saved at all. For my part, I feel the most vile of any creature living; and I am sure sometimes there is not such another existing on this side hell. Now all you can do for me is to pray incessantly that God would make me humble, holy, resigned, and heavenly-minded, by all my trials. *Be strong in the Lord and in the power of His might.* Let us run, wrestle, and fight, that we may win the prize, and obtain that complete happiness, to be holy as God is holy. Wishing and praying that you may advance in learning and grace, and be fit for special service for God, I remain your affectionate brother,

D. B.

To the Same.

KAUNAUMEEK, *December* 27, 1743.

DEAR BROTHER,—I long to see you, and to know how you fare in your journey through a world of inexpressible sorrow, where we are compassed about with vanity, confusion, and vexation of spirit. I am more weary of life, I think, than ever I was. The whole world appears to me like a huge vacuum, a vast empty space, whence nothing desirable or satisfactory can possibly be derived; and I long daily to die more and more to it, even though I obtain not that comfort from spiritual things which I earnestly desire. Worldly pleasures, such as flow from greatness, riches, honours, and sensual gratifications, are infinitely worse than none. May the Lord deliver us more and more from these vanities! I have spent most of the fall and winter hitherto in a very weak state of body, and sometimes under pressing inward trials and spiritual conflicts; but *having obtained help from God, I continue to this day*; and am now something better in health than I was some time ago. I find nothing more conducive to a life of Christianity than a diligent, industrious, and faithful improvement of precious time. Let us then faithfully perform that business which is allotted to us by divine Providence, to the utmost of our bodily strength and mental vigour. Why should we sink and grow discouraged with any

particular trials and perplexities which we are called
to encounter in the world? Death and eternity
are just before us; a few tossing billows more
will waft us into the world of spirits, and we hope
(through infinite grace) into endless pleasures and
uninterrupted rest and peace. Let us then *run with
patience the race set before us.* And O that we could
depend more upon the living God, and less upon
our own wisdom and strength! Dear brother,
may the God of all grace comfort your heart,
succeed your studies, and make you an instrument
of good to His people in your day! This is the
constant prayer of your affectionate brother,

D B

To his Brother Israel, at Haddam.

KAUNAUMEEK, *January* 21, 1743-4.

MY DEAR BROTHER,—There is but one thing
that deserves our highest care and most ardent
desires; and that is, that we may answer the great
end for which we were made, to glorify that God
who has given us our being and all our comforts;
and to do all the good we possibly can to our
fellow-men while we live in the world. Verily,
life is not worth having, if it be not improved for
this noble end and purpose. Yet alas, how little
is this thought of among mankind! Most men
seem to live to themselves, without much regard
to the glory of God or the good of their fellow-

creatures. They earnestly desire and eagerly pursue
after the riches, the honours, and the pleasures
of life, as if they really supposed that wealth,
or greatness, or merriment could make their
immortal souls happy. What false and delusive
dreams are these; and how miserable will those
ere long be who are not awaked out of them,
to see that all their happiness consists in living
to God, and becoming *holy as He is holy*! O,
may you never fall into the tempers and vanities,
the sensuality and folly of the present world!
You are, by divine Providence, left as it were
alone in a wide world, to act for yourself; be sure
then to remember, it is a world of temptation.
You have no earthly parents to be the means of
forming your youth to piety and virtue by their
pious examples and seasonable counsels; let this
then excite you with greater diligence and fervency
to look up to the Father of mercies for grace and
assistance against all the vanities of the world.
And if you would glorify God, answer His just
expectations from you, and make your own soul
happy in this and the coming world, observe these
few directions, though not from a father, yet from
a brother who is touched with a tender concern
for your present and future happiness.

First, Resolve upon and daily endeavour to
practise a life of seriousness and strict sobriety.
The Wise Man will tell you the great advantage
of such a life, Ecclesiastes vii. 3. Think of the

life of Christ; and, when you can find that *He* was pleased with jesting and vain merriment, then you may indulge it in yourself.

Again, Be careful to make a good improvement of precious time. When you cease from labour, fill up your time in reading, meditation, and prayer; and, while your hands are labouring, let your heart be employed, as much as possible, in divine thoughts.

Further, Take heed that you faithfully perform the business you have to do in the world, from a regard to the commands of God; and not from an ambitious desire of being esteemed better than others. We should always look upon ourselves as God's servants, placed in God's world, to do *His* work; and accordingly labour faithfully for Him; not with a design to grow rich and great, but to glorify God and do all the good we possibly can.

Again, Never expect any satisfaction or happiness from the world. If you hope for happiness *in* the world, hope for it from God, and not *from* the world. Do not think you shall be more happy, if you live in such or such a state of life, if you live for yourself; but look upon it that you shall then be happy, when you can be constantly employed for God and not for yourself; and desire to live in this world only to do and suffer what God allots to you. When you can be of the spirit and temper of angels, who are willing to come down into this lower world to perform what

God commands them, though their desires are heavenly and not in the least set on earthly things, then you will be of that temper that you ought to have.

Once more, Never think that you can live to God by your own power or strength; but always look to and rely on Him for assistance, yea, for all strength and grace. There is no greater truth than this, that *we can do nothing of ourselves*; yet nothing but our own experience can effectually teach it to us. Indeed we are a long time in learning that all our strength and salvation is in God. This is a life that I think no unconverted man can possibly live; and yet it is a life that every godly soul is pressing after. Let it then be your great concern thus to devote yourself and your all to God.

I long to see you, that I may say much more to you than I now can for your benefit and welfare. But I desire to commit you to and leave you with the Father of mercies and God of all grace; praying that you may be directed safely through an evil world to God's heavenly kingdom.

D. B.

To a Special Friend.

The Forks of Delaware, *July* 31, 1744.

CERTAINLY the greatest, the noblest pleasure of intelligent creatures must result from their acquaintance with the blessed God, and with their own rational and immortal souls. And O how divinely pleasant and entertaining is it to look into our own souls, when we can find all our powers and passions united and engaged in pursuit after God, our whole souls longing and passionately breathing after a conformity to Him and the full enjoyment of Him! Verily, no hours pass away with so much divine pleasure as those that are spent in communing with God and our own hearts. How sweet is a spirit of devotion, of seriousness and solemnity; a spirit of Gospel simplicity, love, and tenderness! O how desirable and profitable is a spirit of holy watchfulness, and godly jealousy over ourselves; when our souls are afraid of nothing so much as that we shall grieve and offend the blessed God, whom at such times we apprehend, or at least hope, to be a Father and Friend; whom we then love and long to please rather than to be happy ourselves, or at least we delight to derive our happiness from pleasing and glorifying Him. Surely this is a pious temper, worthy of the highest ambition and closest pursuit of intelligent creatures. O how vastly superior is the pleasure, peace, and satisfaction derived from these divine frames, to that which we sometimes seek in things impertinent and trifling! Bitter experience teaches us that *in the midst of such laughter the heart is sorrowful,* and there is no true satisfaction but in God. But alas, how shall we obtain and preserve t his spirit of religion and devotion? Let us follow the apostle's direction, Philippians ii. 12, and labour upon the encouragement he there mentions, for it is God only can afford us this favour ; and He will be sought to, and it is fit we should wait upon Him for so rich a mercy.   May the God of all grace afford us the influences of His Holy Spirit, and help us that we may from our hearts esteem it our greatest liberty and happiness, that *whether we live, we may live to the Lord, or whether we die, we may die to the Lord* ; that in life and death we may be His !

I am in a very poor state of health ; but through divine goodness I am not discontented under my weakness and confinement to this wilderness.   I bless God for this retirement.   I never was more thankful for anything than I have been of late, for the necessity I am under of self-denial in many respects.   I love to be a pilgrim and stranger in this wilderness ; it seems most fit for such a poor ignorant and worthless creature.   I would not change my present mission for any other business in the whole world.   I may tell you freely, without vanity and ostentation, God has of late given me great freedom and fervency in prayer, when I have been so weak and feeble that my nature seemed as if it would speedily dissolve.   I feel as if my *all* was lost, and I was undone for this world, if the poor heathen may not be converted.   In general, I feel different from what I did when I saw you last ; at least more crucified to all the enjoyments of life.   It would be very refreshing to me to see you here in this desert, especially in my weak disconsolate hours; but think I could be content never to see you, or any of my friends again in this world, if God would bless my labours here to the conversion of the poor Indians.

I have much that I could willingly communicate to you, which I must omit, till Providence gives us leave to see each other. In the meantime I remain, D. B.

To a Minister of the Gospel in New Jersey.

The Forks of Delaware, *December* 24, 1744.

Rev. and dear Brother,—I have little to say to you about spiritual joys, and those blessed refreshments and divine consolations with which I have been much favoured in times past; but this I can tell you that, if I gain experience in no other point, yet I am sure I do in this, namely, that the present world has nothing in it to satisfy an immortal soul; and hence that it is not to be desired for itself, but only because God may be seen and served in it; and I wish I could be more patient and willing to live in it for this end than I can usually find myself to be. It is no virtue I know to desire death, only to be freed from the miseries of life; but I want that divine hope which, you observed, when I saw you last, was the very sinews of vital religion. Earth can do us no good, and if there be no hope of our doing good on earth, how can we desire to live in it? Yet we ought to desire, or at least to be resigned, to tarry in it; because it is the will of our all-wise Sovereign. But perhaps these thoughts will appear melancholy and gloomy, and consequently will be very undesirable to you; and therefore I forbear to add. I wish you may not read them in the same circumstances in which I write them. I have a little more to do and suffer in a dark disconsolate world; and then I hope to be as happy as you are. I should ask you to pray for me, were I worth your concern. May the Lord enable us both to *endure hardness as good soldiers of Jesus Christ*; and may we *obtain mercy of God to be faithful to the death,* in the discharge of our respective trusts!—I am, D. B.

## TO HIS BROTHER JOHN AT COLLEGE.

NEW JERSEY, *December* 28, 1745.

VERY DEAR BROTHER,—I am in one continued and uninterrupted hurry; and divine Providence throws so much upon me that I do not see it will ever be otherwise. May I obtain mercy to be found faithful! I cannot say I am weary of my hurry; I only want strength and grace to do more for God than I have ever yet done.

My dear brother, the Lord of heaven, who has carried me through many trials, bless you; bless you for time and eternity; and fit you to serve Him in His Church below, and to enjoy His

blissful presence in His Church triumphant. My
brother, *the time is short.* O let us fill it up for
God; let us *count the sufferings of the present time* as
nothing, if we can but run our race and finish our
course with joy. Let us strive to live to God. I
bless His name that I have nothing to do with
earth, but only to labour honestly in it for God, till
I shall *accomplish as a hireling my day.* I think I
do not desire to live one minute for anything that
earth can afford. O that I could live for none but
God, till my dying moment! D. B.

To his Brother Israel, at Yale College.

Elizabeth Town, New Jersey, *November* 24, 1746.

Dear Brother,—I had determined to make you
and my other friends in New England a visit this
fall; partly from an earnest desire I had to see you
and them, and partly with a view to the recovery
of my health, which has for more than three months
past been much impaired. And in order to prosecute
this design, I set out from my own people about
three weeks ago, and came as far as to this place;
where, my disorder greatly increasing, I have been
obliged to keep house until the day before yesterday, when I was able to ride about half a mile, but
found myself much tired. I have now no hopes
of prosecuting my journey into New England this
winter, supposing my present state of health will
by no means admit of it. I am through divine

goodness much better than I was some days ago,
yet I have not strength now to ride more than ten
miles a day, if the season were warm and fit for
me to travel in. My disorder has been attended
with several symptoms of a consumption; and I
have been at times apprehensive that my great
change was at hand. Yet blessed be God, I have
never been affrighted; but, on the contrary, at
times much delighted with a view of its approach.
O the blessedness of being delivered from the clogs
of flesh and sense, from a body of sin and spiritual
death, and of being translated into a state of
complete purity and perfection! Believe me, my
brother, a lively view and hope of these things will
make the king of terrors himself appear agreeable.
Let me entreat you to keep eternity in view, and
behave yourself as becomes one that must shortly
*give an account of all things done in the body.* That
God may be your God, and prepare you for His
service here and His kingdom of glory hereafter,
is the desire and daily prayer of your affectionate
loving brother,                                        D. B.

To his Brother Israel at College

(written in the time of his extreme illness in
    Boston, a few months before his death).

Boston, *June* 30, 1747.

My dear Brother,—It is from the sides of
eternity I now address you. I am heartily sorry

that I have so little strength to write what I long so much to communicate to you. But let me tell you, my brother, *eternity* is another thing than we ordinarily take it to be in a healthful state. O how vast and boundless; how fixed and unalterable! Of what infinite importance is it, that we be prepared for eternity! I have been just a-dying now for more than a week, and all around me have thought me so; but in this time I have had clear views of eternity. I have seen the blessedness of the godly in some measure, and longed to share their happy state. I have also been comfortably satisfied that through grace I shall do so: but O what anguish is raised in my mind, to think of an eternity for those who are Christless; for those who are mistaken, and who bring their false hopes to the grave with them! The sight was so dreadful that I could by no means bear it. My thoughts recoiled, and I said (but under a more affecting sense than ever before), *Who can dwell with everlasting burnings?* O, if I could but now see my friends, that I might warn them to lay their foundation for eternity sure! And you, my dear brother, I have been particularly concerned for; and have wondered that I so much neglected conversing with you about your spiritual state at our last meeting. O let me then beseech you now to examine whether you are indeed a new creature; whether you have ever acted above self; whether the glory of God has ever been your highest concern; whether you have ever been reconciled to all the perfections of God; in a word, whether God has been your portion, and a holy conformity to Him your chief delight. If you cannot answer positively, consider seriously the frequent breathings of your soul; but do not put yourself off with a slight answer. If you have reason to think you are graceless, O give yourself and the Throne of Grace no rest, till God arise and save. But if the case should be otherwise, bless God for His grace, and press after holiness.

My soul longs that you should be fitted for, and in due time go into the work of the ministry. I cannot bear to think of your going into any other business in life. Do not be discouraged, because you see your elder brothers in the ministry die early, one after another. I declare, now I am dying, I would not have spent my life otherwise for the whole world. But I must leave this with God.

If this line should come to your hands soon after the date, I should be almost desirous you should set out on a journey to me; it may be you may see me alive, which I should much rejoice in. But if you cannot come, I must commit you to the grace of God, where you are. May He be your Guide and Counsellor, your Sanctifier and eternal Portion!

O, my dear brother, flee fleshly lusts, and the enchanting amusements as well as corrupt doctrines of the present day; and strive to live to God. Take this as the *last* line from your affectionate dying brother,                                             D. B.


To a Candidate for the Work of the Ministry.

Very dear Sir,—How amazing it is that *the living who know that they must die* should notwithstanding put far away the evil day, in a season of health and prosperity; and live at such an awful distance from a familiarity with the grave, and the great concerns beyond it. Especially it may justly fill us with surprise, that any whose minds have been divinely enlightened to behold the important things of eternity as they are, I say, that such should live in this manner. And yet, Sir, how frequently is this the case! How rare are the instances of those who live and act, from day to day, as on the verge of eternity; striving to fill up all their remaining moments in the service and to the honour of their great Master! We insensibly trifle away time, while we seem to have enough of it; and are so strangely amused as in a great measure to lose a sense of the holiness and blessed qualifications necessary to prepare us to be inhabitants of the heavenly paradise. But, dear Sir, a dying bed, if we enjoy our reason clearly, will give another view of things. I have now for more than three weeks lain under the greatest degree of weakness, the greater part of

the time expecting daily and hourly to enter into
the eternal world. Sometimes I have been so far
gone as to be wholly speechless for some hours
together; and O, of what vast importance has a
holy spiritual life appeared to me to be in this
season! I have longed to call upon all my friends
to make it their business to live to God; and
especially all that are designed for, or engaged in,
the service of the sanctuary. O, dear Sir, do not
think it enough to live at the rate of common
Christians. Alas, to how little purpose do they
often converse when they meet together! The
visits, even of those who are called Christians
indeed, are frequently very barren; and conscience
cannot but condemn us for the misimprovement of
time while we have been conversant with them.
But the way to enjoy the divine presence, and
be fitted for distinguishing service for God, is to
live a life of great devotion and constant self-
dedication to Him; observing the motions and
dispositions of our own hearts, whence we may
learn the corruptions that lodge there, and our
constant need of help from God for the performance
of the least duty. And, dear Sir, let me beseech
you frequently to attend to the great and precious
duties of secret fasting and prayer.

I have a secret thought, from some things I
have observed, that God may perhaps design you
for some singular service in the world. O then
labour to be prepared and qualified to do much

for God. Read Mr. Edwards's piece on the *Affections*, again and again; and labour to distinguish clearly upon experiences and affections in religion, that you may make a difference between the gold and the shining dross. Labour here, if ever you would be a useful minister of Christ; for nothing has put such a stop to the work of God in the late day as the false religion and wild affections that attended it. Suffer me therefore, finally, to entreat you earnestly to *give yourself to prayer, to reading and meditation*; strive to penetrate to the bottom of divine truths, and never be content with a superficial knowledge. By this means, your thoughts will gradually grow weighty and judicious, and you will possess a valuable treasure, out of which you may produce *things new and old* to the glory of God.

And now I commend you to the grace of God, earnestly desiring that a plentiful portion of the divine Spirit may rest upon you; that you may live to God in every capacity of life, and do abundant service for Him; and that you may be richly qualified for the inheritance of the saints in light.

I scarcely expect to see your face any more in the body, and therefore entreat you to accept this as the last token of love, from your sincerely affectionate dying friend,                    D. B.

*P.S.*—I am now, at the dating of this letter,

considerably recovered from what I was when I wrote it; it having lain by me some time, for want of an opportunity of conveyance; it was written in Boston. I am now able to ride a little, and so am removed into the country; but I have no more expectation of recovering than when I wrote.

To HIS BROTHER JOHN, JUST BEFORE HIS DEATH.

I AM now just on the verge of eternity, expecting very speedily to appear in the unseen world. I feel myself no more an inhabitant of earth, and sometimes earnestly long to *depart and be with Christ.* I bless God, He has for some years given me an abiding conviction that it is impossible for any rational creature to enjoy true happiness without being entirely devoted to Him. Under the influence of this conviction I have in some measure acted : O that I had done more so! I saw both the excellency and necessity of holiness in life; but never in such a manner as now, when I am just brought to the sides of the grave. O, my brother, pursue after holiness; press towards this blessed mark; and let your thirsty soul continually say, *I shall never be satisfied till I awake in Thy likeness.* Although there has been a great deal of selfishness in my views, of which I am ashamed, and for which my soul is humbled; yet blessed be God, I find I have really had, for the most part, such a concern for His glory and the advancement of His kingdom in the world, that it is a satisfaction to me to reflect upon these years.

And now, my dear brother, as I must press you to pursue after personal holiness, to be as much in fasting and prayer as your health will allow, and to live above the rate of common Christians; so I must entreat you solemnly to attend to your public work. Labour to distinguish between true and false religion; and to that end watch the motions of God's Spirit upon your own heart; look to Him for help, and impartially compare your experiences with His Word. Read Mr. Edwards on the *Affections*, where the essence and soul of religion is clearly distinguished from false affections. Value religious joys according to the subject matter of them. There are many who rejoice in their supposed justification; but what do these joys argue except that they love themselves? Whereas, in true spiritual joys, the soul rejoices in God for what He is in Himself; blesses God for His holiness, sovereignty, power, faithfulness, and all His perfections; adores God that He is what He is, that He is unchangeably possessed of infinite glory and happiness. Now, when men thus rejoice in the perfections of God, in the infinite excellency of the way of salvation by Christ, and in the holy commands of God, which are a transcript of His holy nature, these joys are divine and spiritual. Our joys will stand by us at the hour of death, if we can then be satisfied that we have thus acted above self, and in a disinterested manner (if I may so express it) rejoiced in the glory of the blessed God.

I fear you are not sufficiently aware how much false religion there is in the world; many serious Christians and valuable ministers are too easily imposed upon by this false blaze. I likewise fear you are not sensible of the dreadful effects and consequences of this false religion. Let me tell you it is the devil transformed into an angel of light; it is the offspring of hell, that always springs up with every revival of religion, to the injury of the cause of God, while it passes current with multitudes of well-meaning people for the height of religion. Seriously endeavour to crush all appearances of this nature among the Indians, and never encourage any degrees of heat without light. Charge my people in the name of their dying minister, yea, in the name of *Him who was dead and is alive,* to live and walk as becomes the Gospel. Tell them how great the expectations of God and His people are from them, and how awfully they will wound God's cause if they fall into vice, as well as fatally prejudice other poor Indians. Always insist that their experiences are rotten, that their joys are delusive, although they may have been rapt up into the third heavens in their own conceit, unless the main tenor of their lives be spiritual, watchful, and holy. In pressing these things, *thou shalt both save thyself and those that hear thee.*

God knows, I was heartily willing to have served Him longer in the work of the ministry, although it had still been attended with all the labours and hardships of past years, if He had seen fit that it should be so; but as His will now appears otherwise, I am fully content and can with the utmost freedom say, *The will of the Lord be done.* It affects me to think of leaving you in a world of sin; my heart pities you, that those storms and tempests are yet before you, which, I trust, through grace I am almost delivered from. But *God lives, and blessed be my Rock.* He is the same almighty Friend; and will I trust be your Guide and Helper, as He has been mine.

And now, my dear brother, *I commend you to God and to the word of His grace, which is able to build you up, and give you an inheritance among all them that are sanctified.* May you enjoy the divine presence, both in private and public; and may *the arms of your hands be made strong by the mighty God of Jacob!* Which are the passionate desires and prayers of your affectionate dying brother,

D. B.

www.ingramcontent.com/pod-product-compliance
Ingram Content Group UK Ltd.
Pitfield, Milton Keynes, MK11 3LW, UK
UKHW010348140625
459647UK00010B/922